LEISURE ARTS PRESENTS

the Best of
knit
along with

DEBBIE MACOMBER

44 classic designs for family, gifts, and home!

EDITORIAL STAFF

Vice President and Editor-in-Chief: Susan White Sullivan
Knit and Crochet Publications Director:
   Lindsay White Glenn
Special Projects Director: Susan Frantz Wiles
Senior Prepress Director: Mark Hawkins
Art Publications Director: Rhonda Shelby
Technical Writer: Cathy Hardy
Technical Editor: Lois J. Long
Editorial Writer: Susan McManus Johnson
Art Category Manager: Lora Puls
Graphic Artist: Becca Snider
Imaging Technician: Stephanie Johnson
Prepress Technician: Janie Marie Wright
Photography Manager: Katherine Laughlin
Publishing Systems Administrator: Becky Riddle
Mac Information Technology Specialist: Robert Young

BUSINESS STAFF

President and Chief Executive Officer: Rick Barton
Vice President of Sales: Mike Behar
Director of Finance and Administration:
   Laticia Mull Dittrich
National Sales Director: Martha Adams
Creative Services: Chaska Lucas
Information Technology Director: Hermine Linz
Controller: Francis Caple
Vice President, Operations: Jim Dittrich
Retail Customer Service Manager: Stan Raynor
Print Production Manager: Fred F. Pruss

Photo of Debbie Macomber, front cover and page 4, is courtesy of Nina Subin Photography, New York, NY.

TABLE OF contents

3

Dear Friends,

I've often shared with my readers that seeing my first book in print took years of hard work and the continuous support of my family. Some of my readers may not know that, before I could write, I had to gain success at another skill. It was knitting!

My early school years were miserable. I had trouble learning and was at the bottom of my class. I know now that I am dyslexic, but back then, they just thought I was a slow learner. I had no self-esteem, and all the negative messages I kept hearing had a profound effect on me. I had no faith that I could do anything. I desperately needed a confidence boost!

For some reason, when I was eleven, I begged my mother to let me have yarn and knitting needles. She took me to a yarn shop, and the ladies there showed me the basic stitches.

Finally, I knew something no one at school knew! I began teaching my classmates how to knit, and it did wonders for my self-esteem. My reading and math skills improved. I enjoyed a sense of accomplishment, which was new to me. One of my fondest memories of junior high was the fashion show of all the clothing I had knitted.

Years later, with countless sweaters, scarves, and hats completed and dozens of my books on the shelf, I began to add knitting to my stories. Many of you noticed that my characters relax with knitting. You've told me how these stories resonate with you, because you also knit. In that wonderful way of one good thing leading to another, this series of knitting pattern books followed.

I've loved hearing how much you've enjoyed the baby blankets, garments, and accessories in the eleven *Knit Along with Debbie Macomber* pattern books. Your feedback gave me an idea: Why not take some of our favorite patterns from each book and put them together in *The Best of Knit Along with Debbie Macomber*? My Blossom Street and Cedar Cove stories were the inspiration for many of the patterns included in this new volume, while others were featured in *Debbie's Favorites*, *Friendship Shawls*, and *A Charity Guide for Knitters*.

Like so many knitters, I do believe it's important to help others. That's why I've donated the proceeds from sales of my Knit Along books to knitting charities. To help you with your volunteer projects, seventeen of the Warm Up America! blocks from the pattern books are here. They're perfect for making cozy sampler afghans for those in need.

And of course, you already know another way your love of knitting can help. Teach someone else how to knit—it truly can make all the difference!

Debbie

Knitting that everyone can enjoy—these very special accessories for the home will add warmth and comfort to every room. And each design is perfect for gift-giving. Enjoy knitting these thoughtful lap throws, pretty pillows, and a sweet spa set.

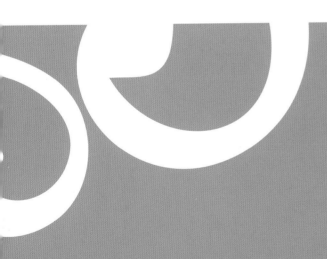

home

two-tone throw

In Debbie's book Twenty Wishes, *Anne Marie Roche owns a bookstore on Blossom Street. Recently widowed, Anne Marie decides to allay her grief by helping eight-year-old Ellen overcome her shyness. When Ellen's grandmother becomes ill, Anne Marie knits a warm lap throw to help with her recovery.*

 EASY

Finished Size: 32¹/₂" x 48" (82.5 cm x 122 cm)

MATERIALS

Bulky Weight Yarn **BULKY 5**
[3.5 ounces, 148 yards
(100 grams, 136 meters) per skein]:
    Taupe - 5 skeins
    Black - 4 skeins
29" (73.5 cm) Circular knitting needle,
    size 10¹/₂ (6.5 mm) **or** size needed for gauge

GAUGE: In pattern, 14 sts = 3³/₄" (9.5 cm)
        and 24 rows = 3¹/₂" (9 cm)

THROW

With Taupe cast on 121 sts.

Rows 1 and 2: With Taupe, knit across.

When instructed to slip a stitch, always slip as if to **purl** with yarn held on the **wrong** side.

Row 3 (Right side): With Black, K3, slip 1, (K1, slip 1) across to last 3 sts, K3.

Row 4: K3, with yarn forward slip 1, (K1, with yarn forward slip 1) across to last 3 sts, K3.

Repeat Rows 1-4 for pattern until piece measures approximately 48" (122 cm) from cast on edge, ending by working Row 2.

Bind off all sts in **knit**.

sculptured pillows

Michael Everett's wife Hannah always got the last word—even after she passed away. These beautiful pillows could very well have been knitted by Hannah's cousin, Winter. And since Michael has no idea how to approach Winter about the contents of Hannah's final letter, he'll just have to use Hannah's belongings as an excuse. Read Debbie's book Hannah's List *to find out if Hannah's final wishes come true.*

Finished Size: 12" (30.5 cm) square

MATERIALS
Medium Weight Yarn 4
[3.5 ounces, 220 yards
(100 grams, 201 meters) per hank]:
   2 hanks for **each** Pillow
16" (40.5 cm) **and** 24" (61 cm) Circular
   knitting needles, size 8 (5 mm) **or** size
   needed for gauge
Cable needle (for Traveling Cables)
Markers
Yarn needle
Pillow form(s) - 12" (30.5 cm) square **each**

Techniques used:
• K2 tog *(Fig. 11, page 196)*
• SSK *(Figs. 13a-c, page 196)*

GAUGE: In Stockinette Stitch,
          18 sts and 24 rnds = 4" (10 cm)

Each Square is knit in the round *(see Using Circular Needle, page 192).*

Tip: As the stitch count decreases and the rounds become smaller, change to 16" (40.5 cm) circular knitting needle.

Tip: To achieve even corner miters, it is important to keep good tension. After working a decrease, insert the needle into the next stitch and tighten by pulling firmly on the working yarn, then complete the stitch.

8 POINT FLOWER
◼◼◻◻ **EASY**

SQUARE (Make 2)
Using 24" (61 cm) circular knitting needle, ★ cast on 54 sts, place marker *(see Markers, page 191)*; repeat from ★ 3 times **more**: 216 sts.

Note: The last marker placed indicates the beginning of the round.

Rnd 1 (Right side - Decrease rnd)**:** ★ K2 tog, knit across to within 2 sts of next marker, SSK; repeat from ★ around: 208 sts.

Rnd 2: Purl around.

Rnd 3: Repeat Rnd 1: 200 sts.

Rnd 4: Purl around.

Instructions continued on page 12.

Rnds 5-7: Repeat Rnd 1, 3 times: 176 sts.

Rnd 8: Knit around.

Rnd 9: Repeat Rnd 1: 168 sts.

Rnds 10 and 11: Purl around.

Rnds 12-14: Repeat Rnd 1, 3 times: 144 sts.

Rnd 15: Knit around.

Rnd 16: Repeat Rnd 1: 136 sts.

Rnds 17-19: Purl around.

Rnds 20-22: Repeat Rnd 1, 3 times: 112 sts.

Rnd 23: Knit around.

Rnd 24: Repeat Rnd 1: 104 sts.

Rnd 25: Purl around.

Rnds 26-28: Repeat Rnd 1, 3 times: 80 sts.

Rnd 29: Knit around.

Rnd 30: Repeat Rnd 1: 72 sts.

Rnds 31-33: Purl around.

Rnds 34 and 35: Repeat Rnd 1 twice: 56 sts.

Rnd 36: Keeping first marker in place to indicate beginning of rnd, knit around removing remaining markers.

Rnds 37-45: Knit around.

Rnd 46: Purl around.

Rnd 47: Knit around.

Rnd 48: Purl around.

Cut yarn leaving a long end, then push yarn end through center opening to the **wrong** side.

CENTER WEAVING

This procedure allows the design to become dimensional. Slide all of the stitches onto the cable portion of the circular needle. This allows room for the yarn needle to pass through the stitches more easily.

RIGHT SIDE

Thread the yarn needle with an 18" (45.5 cm) length of yarn.

With **right** side of Square facing and working from **right** to **left** (as if to purl), insert the yarn needle through the stitches as follows:

8 Point Flower - Insert needle through first 2 sts, skip next 3 sts, (insert needle through next 4 sts, skip next 3 sts) 7 times, insert needle through last 2 sts.

Pull the yarn through, leaving a 3" (7.5 cm) end at the beginning; remove the yarn needle.

WRONG SIDE
Rethread the yarn needle with an 18" (45.5 cm) length of yarn.
With **right** side of piece facing, roll the stitches forward to expose the **wrong** side of the stitches; working from **right** to **left**, weave the yarn through the stitches as follows:

8 Point Flower - Skip first 2 sts, insert needle through next 3 sts, (skip next 4 sts, insert needle through next 3 sts) 7 times, skip last 2 sts.

Pull the yarn through, leaving a 3" (7.5 cm) end at the beginning; remove the yarn needle.

Make sure the yarn has been woven through **each** stitch, then remove the circular needle.

Push the wrong side yarn ends through the center opening and turn the square over. Gather all wrong side stitches up tightly by pulling on the yarn ends; tie a knot.

Turn the square over and gather all right side stitches tightly by pulling on the yarn ends; tie a knot.
Thread the yarn needle with the right side yarn ends and pass through the center to the wrong side. Turn the square over and tie all of the yarn ends together. Weave in all the ends on wrong side.

This gathering process creates ridges with the right side stitches and valleys with the wrong side stitches. Using the photo as a guide, sculpt your squares by gently shaping the ridges and the valleys.

ASSEMBLY
With **wrong** sides together and working through **both** loops of cast on edge on **both** Squares, sew pieces together forming a ridge and inserting pillow form before closing.

Instructions continued on page 14.

TRAVELING CABLES

■■■◻ INTERMEDIATE

STITCH GUIDE

FRONT CABLE (uses 4 sts)
Slip next 2 sts onto cable needle and hold in **front** of work, K2 from left needle, K2 from cable needle.

BACK CABLE (uses 4 sts)
Slip next 2 sts onto cable needle and hold in **back** of work, K2 from left needle, K2 from cable needle.

SQUARE (Make 2)

Work same as 8 Point Flower, page 10, through Rnd 33: 72 sts.

Rnd 34: Repeat Rnd 1: 64 sts.

Rnd 35: (Work Front Cable, K8, work Back Cable) around.

Rnds 36 and 37: Knit around.

Rnd 38: K2, work Front Cable, K4, work Back Cable, ★ K4, work Front Cable, K4, work Back Cable; repeat from ★ 2 times **more**, K2.

Rnds 39 and 40: Knit around.

Rnd 41: K4, work Front Cable, work Back Cable, (K8, work Front Cable, work Back Cable) 3 times, K4.

Rnds 42 and 43: Knit around.

Rnds 44 and 45: Repeat Rnd 1 twice: 48 sts.

Rnd 46: Keeping first marker in place to indicate beginning of rnd, knit around removing remaining markers.

Rnds 47 and 48: Knit around.

Cut yarn leaving a long end, then push yarn end through center opening to the **wrong** side.

CENTER WEAVING

Work same as 8 Point Flower, page 12, working through stitches as follows:

Right side of Traveling Cable - Skip first 3 sts, insert needle through next 6 sts, (skip next 6 sts, insert needle through next 6 sts) 3 times, skip last 3 sts.

Wrong side of Traveling Cable - Insert needle through first 3 sts, skip next 6 sts, (insert needle through next 6 sts, skip next 6 sts) 3 times, insert needle through last 3 sts.

ASSEMBLY

With **wrong** sides together and working through **both** loops of cast on edge on **both** Squares, sew pieces together forming a ridge and inserting pillow form before closing.

Designs by Leslie Calaway.

pretty panels afghan

As Anne Marie Roche of Twenty Wishes finishes each knitting project, she's already planning another. She'll be moving out of her tiny apartment over the bookstore soon. This gorgeous afghan is one she's making for her new home, the one she and her little dog Baxter will share with someone who means the world to her.

Shown on page 17.

■■□□ EASY

Finished Size: 46¹/₂" x 66" (118 cm x 167.5 cm)

MATERIALS

Bulky Weight Yarn [5]
[3 ounces, 135 yards
(85 grams, 123 meters) per skein]:
  Rose - 7 skeins
  Brown - 4 skeins
Straight knitting needles, size 11 (8 mm)
  or size needed for gauge
Cable needle
Yarn needle

GAUGE: In Stockinette Stitch,
  11 sts and 16 rows = 4" (10 cm)

Techniques used:
- YO (*Fig. 5a, page 194*)
- M1 (*Figs. 10a & b, page 196*)
- K2 tog (*Fig. 11, page 196*)
- slip 1, K1, PSSO (*Figs. 14a & b, page 197*)

LACE PANEL (Make 3)

Finished Width: 10¹/₂" (26.5 cm)

With Rose, cast on 29 sts.

Row 1 (Right side)**:** K1, (P1, K1) across.

Always slip the first stitch as if to **purl** with yarn forward.

Rows 2-4: Slip 1, (P1, K1) across.

Row 5: Slip 1, P1, K 25, P1, K1.

Instructions continued on page 16.

Row 6 AND ALL WRONG SIDE ROWS: Slip 1, P1, K1, P 23, K1, P1, K1.

Row 7: Slip 1, P1, K 25, P1, K1.

Row 9: Slip 1, P1, K 10, K2 tog, YO, K1, YO, slip 1 as if to **knit**, K1, PSSO, K 10, P1, K1.

Row 11: Slip 1, P1, K9, K2 tog, YO, K3, YO, slip 1 as if to **knit**, K1, PSSO, K9, P1, K1.

Row 13: Slip 1, P1, K8, (K2 tog, YO) twice, K1, (YO, slip 1 as if to **knit**, K1, PSSO) twice, K8, P1, K1.

Row 15: Slip 1, P1, K7, (K2 tog, YO) twice, K3, (YO, slip 1 as if to **knit**, K1, PSSO) twice, K7, P1, K1.

Row 17: Slip 1, P1, K6, (K2 tog, YO) 3 times, K1, (YO, slip 1 as if to **knit**, K1, PSSO) 3 times, K6, P1, K1.

Rows 18-260: Repeat Rows 6-17, 20 times; then repeat Rows 6-8 once **more**.

Rows 261-264: Slip 1, (P1, K1) across.

Bind off all sts in pattern.

CABLE PANEL (Make 2)
Finished Width: 7¹/₂" (19 cm)

With Brown, cast on 22 sts.

Row 1 (Right side): (K1, P1) across.

Note: Always slip the first stitch as if to **purl** with yarn forward.

Row 2: Slip 1, K1, (P1, K1) across.

Row 3: Slip 1, P1, (K1, P1) across to last 2 sts, K2.

Row 4: Slip 1, K1, (P1, K1) across.

Row 5: Slip 1, P2, K2, P3, K2, (M1, K2) twice, P3, K2, P1, K2: 24 sts.

Row 6: Slip 1, K2, P2, K3, P8, K3, P2, K1, P1, K1.

Row 7: Slip 1, P2, K2, P3, K8, P3, K2, P1, K2.

Row 8: Slip 1, K2, P2, K3, P8, K3, P2, K1, P1, K1.

To work Cable (uses 8 sts), slip next 4 stitches onto cable needle and hold in **front** of work, K4 from left needle, K4 from cable needle.

Row 9: Slip 1, P2, K2, P3, work Cable, P3, K2, P1, K2.

Row 10: Slip 1, K2, P2, K3, P8, K3, P2, K1, P1, K1.

Rows 11-16: Repeat Rows 7 and 8, 3 times.

Rows 17-260: Repeat Rows 9-16, 30 times; then repeat Rows 9-12 once **more**.

Row 261: Slip 1, P2, K2, P3, K2, K2 tog twice, K2, P3, K2, P1, K2: 22 sts.

Row 262: Slip 1, K1, (P1, K1) across.

Row 263: Slip 1, P1, (K1, P1) across to last 2 sts, K2.

Rows 264 and 265: Repeat Rows 262 and 263.

Bind off all sts in pattern.

ASSEMBLY
Whipstitch Panels together *(Fig. 24, page 199)*, placing cast on edge of each Panel at the same end and alternating Lace and Cable Panels.

Design by Cathy Hardy.

keepsake doily

In Twenty Wishes, Anne Marie Roche is delighted when Lydia, the yarn shop owner, offers the use of this lovely doily for a party decoration. Knit using cotton thread, it starts with a crochet-hook cast-on and ends with delicate chained loops all around.

■■■□ **INTERMEDIATE**

Finished Size: 13" (33 cm) diameter

MATERIALS

Bedspread Weight Cotton Thread (size 10) [1,000 yards (914 meters) per ball]:
    1 ball
4 Double pointed knitting needles,
    size 1(2.25 mm) **or** size needed for gauge
Steel crochet hook, size 4 (2 mm)
Rust proof straight pins or T pins
Blocking board
Spray starch or fabric stiffener

GAUGE: In Stockinette Stitch,
        18 sts and 24 rows = 2" (5 cm)

Gauge Swatch: 3¹/₂" (9 cm) diameter
Work same as Doily through Rnd 19.

Techniques used:
• YO *(Fig. 5a, page 194)*
• slip 1, K1, PSSO *(Figs. 14a & b, page 197)*
• slip 1, K2 tog, PSSO *(Fig. 16, page 197)*

DOILY

Make a beginning loop as follows: Wrap the thread clockwise around your left index finger twice. Insert the crochet hook under both strands, yarn over (by bringing the thread over the top of the hook from back to front) *(Fig. A)* and pull thread through loop, yarn over and pull thread through the stitch on the hook (**counts as first cast on stitch**); remove finger from loop.

For next cast on stitch: yarn over, insert hook in loop, yarn over and pull thread through loop, yarn over and draw through 2 loops on hook *(Fig. B)*.

Fig. A

Fig. B

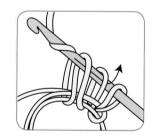

Instructions continued on page 20.

Crochet cast on a total of 6 sts and transfer 2 sts to each of 3 needles (see Double Pointed Needles, page 193).

Rnd 1 (Right side): (K1, YO) across each needle: 4 sts each needle; 12 sts total.

Rnds 2-4: Knit around.

Rnd 5: (K1, YO) across each needle: 8 sts each needle; 24 sts total.

Rnds 6-8: Knit around.

Rnd 9: (K1, YO twice) across each needle: 24 sts each needle; 72 sts total.

Rnd 10: (K2, P1) across each needle.

Rnds 11 and 12: Knit around.

When instructed to slip a stitch that will be used in a decrease, always slip as if to **knit**.

Rnd 13: ★ K3, slip 1, K1, PSSO, K3, YO; repeat from ★ across each needle.

Rnd 14 AND ALL EVEN NUMBERED RNDS: Knit around.

Rnd 15: ★ K2, slip 1, K2 tog, PSSO, K2, YO, K1, YO; repeat from ★ across each needle.

Rnd 17: ★ K1, slip 1, K2 tog, PSSO, K1, YO, K3, YO; repeat from ★ across each needle.

Rnd 19: ★ Slip 1, K2 tog, PSSO, YO, K2 tog, YO, K1, YO, slip 1, K1, PSSO, YO; repeat from ★ across each needle.

Rnd 21: (K1, YO) across each needle: 48 sts each needle; 144 sts total.

Rnd 23: ★ YO, K1, YO, K6, slip 1, K2 tog, PSSO, K6; repeat from ★ across each needle.

Rnd 25: ★ YO, K3, YO, K5, slip 1, K2 tog, PSSO, K5; repeat from ★ across each needle.

Rnd 27: ★ YO, K2 tog, YO, K1, YO, slip 1, K1, PSSO, YO, K4, slip 1, K2 tog, PSSO, K4; repeat from ★ across each needle.

Rnd 29: ★ YO, K2 tog, YO, K3, YO, slip 1, K1, PSSO, YO, K3, slip 1, K2 tog, PSSO, K3; repeat from ★ across each needle.

Rnd 31: ★ (YO, K2 tog) twice, YO, K1, YO, (slip 1, K1, PSSO, YO) twice, K2, slip 1, K2 tog, PSSO, K2; repeat from ★ across each needle.

Rnd 33: ★ (YO, K2 tog) twice, YO, K3, YO, (slip 1, K1, PSSO, YO) twice, K1, slip 1, K2 tog, PSSO, K1; repeat from ★ across each needle.

Rnd 35: ★ (YO, K2 tog) 3 times, YO, K1, YO, (slip 1, K1, PSSO, YO) 3 times, slip 1, K2 tog, PSSO; repeat from ★ across each needle.

Rnd 37: (K1, YO) across each needle: 96 sts each needle; 288 sts total.

Rnd 39: ★ K 13, slip 1, K2 tog, PSSO, K 13, YO, K3, YO; repeat from ★ across each needle.

Rnd 41: ★ K 12, slip 1, K2 tog, PSSO, K 12, YO, K5, YO; repeat from ★ across each needle.

Rnd 43: ★ K 11, slip 1, K2 tog, PSSO, K 11, YO, K7, YO; repeat from ★ across each needle.

Rnd 45: ★ K 10, slip 1, K2 tog, PSSO, K 10, YO, K9, YO; repeat from ★ across each needle.

Rnd 47: ★ K9, slip 1, K2 tog, PSSO, K9, YO, K 11, YO; repeat from ★ across each needle.

Rnd 49: ★ K8, slip 1, K2 tog, PSSO, K8, YO, K 13, YO; repeat from ★ across each needle.

Rnd 51: ★ K7, slip 1, K2 tog, PSSO, K7, YO, K 15, YO; repeat from ★ across each needle.

Rnd 53: ★ K6, slip 1, K2 tog, PSSO, K6, YO, K 17, YO; repeat from ★ across each needle.

Rnd 55: ★ K5, slip 1, K2 tog, PSSO, K5, YO, K 19, YO; repeat from ★ across each needle.

Rnd 57: ★ K4, slip 1, K2 tog, PSSO, K4, YO, K 21, YO; repeat from ★ across each needle.

Rnd 59: ★ K3, slip 1, K2 tog, PSSO, K3, YO, K 23, YO; repeat from ★ across each needle.

Rnd 61: ★ K2, slip 1, K2 tog, PSSO, K2, YO, K 25, YO; repeat from ★ across each needle.

Rnd 63: ★ K1, slip 1, K2 tog, PSSO, K1, YO, K 27, YO; repeat from ★ across each needle.

Rnd 65: ★ Slip 1, K2 tog, PSSO, YO, K 29, YO; repeat from ★ across each needle.

To make a chain: Yarn over and draw the thread through the stitch on the hook (*Fig. C*); repeat for each chain required.

Fig. C

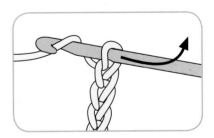

Instructions continued on page 22.

To work off sts: Insert hook through 3 sts on left needle *(Fig. D)* and slip them off the needle, YO and draw through all loops on hook.

Fig. D

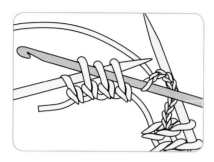

Rnd 67: Slip 1 st from the right needle to the left needle, insert crochet hook in last st on right needle *(Fig. E)*, ★ (chain 10, work off 3 sts) 5 times, chain 10, work off 5 sts, (chain 10, work off 3 sts) 4 times; repeat from ★ across each needle; insert hook in first chain of beginning chain 10, YO and draw through st and loop on hook.

Fig. E

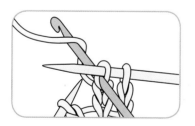

Wash and block Doily as follows:
Using a mild detergent and warm water and being careful not to rub, twist, or wring, gently squeeze suds through the piece. Rinse several times in cool, clear water. Roll piece in a clean terry towel and gently press out the excess moisture. Lay piece on a flat surface and shape to proper size; where needed, pin in place using rust-proof pins. Allow to dry **completely**.

Spray **wrong** side of Doily lightly with starch or fabric stiffener. Spread Doily on blocking board and stretch to shape; pin chain loops in place until dry.

Design by Larisa Scott.

spa cloth & soap sack

Three generations of women are headed for adventure—and maybe romance—in Debbie's book A Turn in the Road. *Bethanne Hamlin is making the journey with her heartbroken daughter and her ex-mother-in-law. Bethanne takes along these little luxuries, because after a long day on the road with well-intentioned family, nothing is more restorative than a nice soak in the tub.*

Shown on page 25.

◼◼◻◻ **EASY**

Finished Sizes
Spa Cloth: 8"w x 8³/₄"h (20.5 cm x 22 cm)
Soap Sack: 6" circumference x 5³/₄" tall
(15 cm x 14.5 cm)

MATERIALS
100% Cotton Medium Weight Yarn
[1.75 ounces, 80 yards
(50 grams, 73 meters) per skein**]:**
    2 skeins
Straight knitting needles, size 7 (4.5 mm) **or**
    size needed for gauge
Yarn needle
¹/₈" (3 mm) wide Ribbon - 18" (45.5 cm) length

GAUGE: In Stockinette Stitch (knit one row,
            purl one row),
            17 sts and 26 rows = 4" (10 cm)

Techniques used:
• YO *(Figs. 5a & b, page 194)*
• knit increase *(Figs. 7a & b, page 195)*
• K2 tog *(Fig. 11, page 196)*
• slip 1, K2, PSSO *(Fig. 15, page 197)*

SPA CLOTH
Cast on 42 sts.

Row 1: Knit across.

Row 2 (Right side): P2, (slip 1 as if to **knit**, K2, PSSO, P2) across: 34 sts.

Row 3: K2, (P1, YO, P1, K2) across: 42 sts.

Row 4: P2, (K3, P2) across.

Row 5: K2, (P3, K2) across.

Rows 6-12: Repeat Rows 2-5 once, then repeat Rows 2-4 once **more**.

Instructions continued on page 24.

Row 13: (K2, P3) twice, K 22, (P3, K2) twice.

Row 14: P2, (slip 1 as if to **knit**, K2, PSSO, P2) twice, K 18, P2, (slip 1 as if to **knit**, K2, PSSO, P2) twice: 38 sts.

Row 15: (K2, P1, YO, P1) twice, K3, P 16, K3, (P1, YO, P1, K2) twice: 42 sts.

Row 16: P2, (K3, P2) twice, K 18, P2, (K3, P2) twice.

Row 17: (K2, P3) twice, K3, P 16, K3, (P3, K2) twice.

Rows 18-44: Repeat Rows 14-17, 6 times; then repeat Rows 14-16 once **more**.

Row 45: (K2, P3) twice, K 22, (P3, K2) twice.

Rows 46-58: Repeat Rows 2-5, 3 times; then repeat Row 2 once **more**.

Bind off all sts in **knit**.

SOAP SACK

Cast on 16 sts.

Row 1 (Right side): Increase in each st across: 32 sts.

Row 2: K2, (P3, K2) across.

Row 3: P2, (slip 1 as if to **knit**, K2, PSSO, P2) across: 26 sts.

Row 4: K2, (P1, YO, P1, K2) across: 32 sts.

Row 5: P2, (K3, P2) across.

Rows 6-30: Repeat Rows 2-5, 6 times; then repeat Row 2 once **more**.

Row 31 (Eyelet row): K2, (YO, K2 tog) across to last 2 sts, K2.

Row 32: Purl across.

Row 33: Increase in each st across: 64 sts.

Row 34: Purl across.

Row 35: Knit across.

Row 36: Purl across.

Bind off all sts in **knit**, leaving a long end for sewing.

Weave seam *(Fig. 23, page 199)*, then weave yarn through cast on sts, gather tightly and secure end.

Weave ribbon through Eyelet row for drawstring.

Design by Rhonda White.

garter stitch squares

This striking afghan is from Debbie's Favorites. The squares are joined in a unique and sturdy way, with lengths of crocheted chains. Debbie says, "The contrast on this afghan is interesting—the solid and striped garter stitch squares and whipstitched edgings all come together to make a bold statement."

◼◼◼◻ INTERMEDIATE

Finished Size: 48" x 67" (122 cm x 170 cm)

MATERIALS

Medium Weight Yarn
[3¹/₂ ounces, 223 yards
(100 grams, 204 meters) per skein]:
   Black - 12 skeins
   White - 4 skeins
Straight knitting needles, size 9 (5.5 mm) **or**
   size needed for gauge
Crochet hook, size G (4.5 mm) **or** size
   needed for gauge
Yarn needle

GAUGE: In Garter Stitch, 16 sts and
32 rows (16 ridges) = 4" (10 cm)
Crocheted Edging, 16 sc = 4" (10 cm)
One Square = 9¹/₂" (24 cm) square

SOLID SQUARE (Make 18)

With Black, cast on 32 sts.

Rows 1-60: Knit across (Garter Stitch): 30 ridges.

Bind off all sts; do **not** cut yarn **or** finish off.

Note: Loop a short piece of yarn around the **back** of any stitch on Row 60 to mark **right** side and **top** of square.

CROCHETED EDGING
See Basic Crochet Stitches, page 203.

Rnd 1: Transfer remaining loop to crochet hook; ch 1, with **right** side facing, (sc, ch 2, sc) in corner, work 29 sc evenly spaced along each side working (sc, ch 2, sc) in each corner; join with slip st to first sc: 124 sc and 4 ch-2 sps.

Rnd 2 (Eyelet rnd): (Slip st, ch 6, dc) in first ch-2 sp, ch 1, skip next sc, (dc in next sc, ch 1, skip next sc) 15 times, ★ (dc, ch 3, dc) in next ch-2 sp, ch 1, skip next sc, (dc in next sc, ch 1, skip next sc) 15 times; repeat from ★ 2 times **more**; join with slip st to third ch of beginning ch-6, finish off.

Instructions continued on page 28.

STRIPED SQUARE (Make 17)

With Black, cast on 32 sts.

Do **not** cut yarn; carry yarn **loosely** along the sides when not being used.

Rows 1-4: With White, knit across.

Rows 5-8: With Black, knit across.

Rows 9-60: Repeat Rows 1-8, 6 times; then repeat Rows 1-4 once **more**.

Cut White; with Black bind off all sts; do **not** cut yarn **or** finish off.

Note: Loop a short piece of yarn around the **back** of any stitch on Row 60 to mark **right** side and **top** of square.

CROCHETED EDGING

Work same as Solid Square.

FINISHING
ASSEMBLY

Afghan is assembled by joining 7 Squares into 5 vertical Strips and then by joining Strips.

Lay out Squares, with all marked edges at the top, referring to the Placement Diagram.

PLACEMENT DIAGRAM

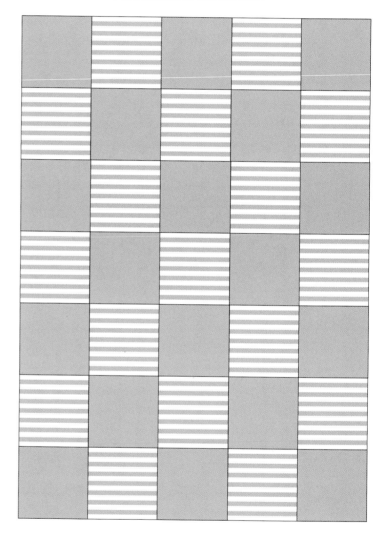

Place two Squares with **wrong** sides together. With Black and beginning in center of corner ch, sew through both pieces once to secure the beginning of the seam, leaving an ample yarn end to weave in later. Insert the needle from **front** to **back** through **inside** loops only of each stitch on **both** pieces *(Fig. A)*. Bring the needle around and insert it from **front** to **back** through the next loops of both pieces. Continue in this manner across to center of next corner ch, keeping the sewing yarn fairly loose.

Whipstitch Strips together in the same manner.

Always working in the same direction, repeat 7 times, working between Squares **and** across both ends of Afghan.

Fig. B

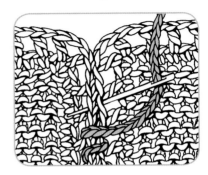

VERTICAL CHAINS

With White, chain a 155" (394 cm) length; do **not** finish off.

Thread beginning end through yarn needle.

Weave Chain through vertical eyelets in same manner as Horizontal Chains.

Note: Chains should form an "X" at intersections.

Fig. A

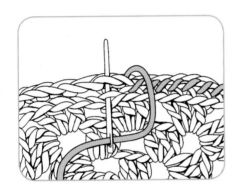

HORIZONTAL CHAINS

With White, chain a 115" (292 cm) length; do **not** finish off.

Thread beginning end through yarn needle.

Weave Chain through horizontal eyelets between Squares in same manner as whipstitching *(Fig. B)*, adjust length of chain if necessary; finish off and secure both ends.

Repeat 5 times, working between Squares **and** along both sides of Afghan.

Designed by Marion Graham.

Ask a knitter to name a favorite project, and you may hear about the world's best baby gift. What makes each knitted gift so very special is no mystery at all—it's knitted for the world's best baby, of course! There are several sweet baby items in the *Knit Along With Debbie Macomber* pattern books. Here are a few of those darling designs—and it was difficult to choose only a few!

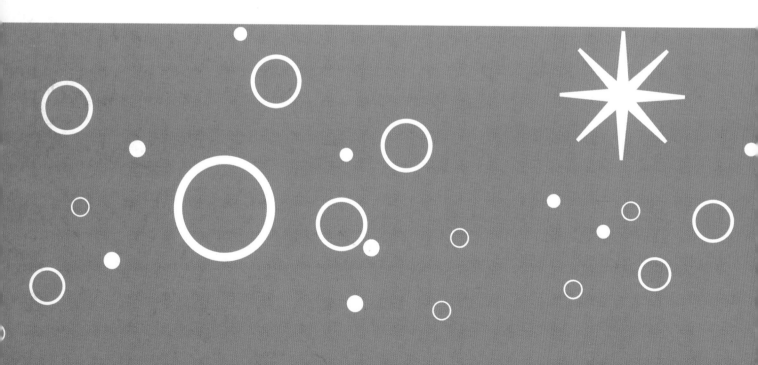

baby

springtime pullover

The pullover this little darling is wearing is from Debbie's Favorites. Debbie explains, "Lisa Ellis is one of my talented knitting friends, and this sweet little sweater is one of her designs. I love the tulip front and bright color-block sleeves and back."

■■■□ **INTERMEDIATE**

Size	Finished Chest Measurement
X-Small (3-6 mo)	19" (48.5 cm)
Small (6-12 mo)	21¼" (54 cm)
Medium (1-2 Toddler)	24" (61 cm)
Large (2-3 Toddler)	26¼" (66.5 cm)

Size Note: Instructions are written for size X-Small with sizes Small, Medium and Large in braces { }. Instructions will be easier to read if you circle all the numbers pertaining to your child's size. If only one number is given, it applies to all sizes.

MATERIALS

Light Weight Yarn 🄯 **3**
[1¾ ounces, 190 yards
(50 grams, 174 meters) per skein]:
    Pink, Purple, Yellow, and Green -
    1 skein of **each** color
Straight knitting needles, size 6 (4 mm) **or**
    size needed for gauge
16" (40.5 cm) Circular knitting needle,
    size 6 (4 mm) **or** size needed for gauge
Double-pointed knitting needles,
    size 6 (4 mm) (for 3-Needle Bind Off)
Stitch holders - 4
Bobbins - optional
Markers
7/16" (11 mm) Button - 1
Yarn needle

GAUGE: In Stockinette Stitch,
    22 sts and 32 rows = 4" (10 cm)

Techniques used:
• changing colors (*Figs. 3a & b, page 193*)
• YO (*Fig. 5a, page 194*)
• adding new sts (*Figs. 6a & b, page 195*)
• K2 tog (*Fig. 11, page 196*)
• SSK (*Figs. 13a-c, page 196*)

FRONT
BAND
With straight knitting needles and Pink, cast on 55{61-69-75} sts.

Work in Garter Stitch (knit every row), until Band measures approximately 1" (2.5 cm).

BODY
Work in Stockinette Stitch (knit one row, purl one row) until Front measures approximately 5{5½-7-8½}"/12.5{14-18-21.5} cm from cast on edge, ending by working a **purl** row.

Instructions continued on page 34.

FOLLOWING A CHART

The chart shows each stitch as a square indicating what color each stitch should be. Visualize the chart as your fabric, beginning at the bottom edge. Place a ruler above the row you are knitting.

On **right** side rows, follow chart from **right** to **left**; on **wrong** side rows, follow chart from **left** to **right**.

FLOWER CHART

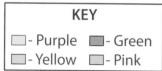

Row
-20

-11

-1 (Right side)

KEY
☐ - Purple   ■ - Green
☐ - Yellow   ☐ - Pink

Next Row: K 20{23-27-30}, place a marker *(see Markers, page 191)*, with Purple, work Row 1 of Flower Chart, place a marker, K 20{23-27-30}.

Next 3 Rows: Work across to next marker, work next row of Flower Chart, work across.

ARMHOLE SHAPING
Maintain established pattern throughout.

Rows 1 and 2: Bind off 3{3-4-4} sts at beginning of next 2 rows, work across working Flower Chart between markers: 49{55-61-67} sts.

Next 16 Rows: Work across, working Flower Chart between markers.

With Pink and removing markers, work even until Armholes measure approximately 2½{3-2½-3}"/6.5{7.5-6.5-7.5} cm, ending by working a **purl** row.

NECK SHAPING
Both sides of the Neck are worked at the same time, using separate yarn for **each** side.

Row 1: K 20{22-24-26}, bind off 9{11-13-15} sts; with second yarn, knit across: 20{22-24-26} sts **each** side.

Row 2: Purl across; with second yarn, purl across.

Row 3 (Decrease row)**:** Knit across to within 3 sts of Neck edge, K2 tog, K1; with second yarn, K1, SSK, knit across: 19{21-23-25} sts **each** side.

Rows 4-9: Repeat Rows 2 and 3, 3 times: 16{18-20-22} sts **each** side.

Work even until Armholes measure approximately 4{4¹/₂-4¹/₂-5}"/10{11.5-11.5-12.5} cm, ending by working a **purl** row.

Place sts from each shoulder onto st holders for 3-Needle Bind Off.

BACK
BAND
With straight knitting needles and Purple, cast on 54{60-68-74} sts.

Work in Garter Stitch, until Band measures approximately 1" (2.5 cm).

BODY
Work in Stockinette Stitch until Back measures same as Front to Armhole Shaping, ending by working a **purl** row.

ARMHOLE SHAPING
Maintain established pattern throughout.

Rows 1 and 2: Bind off 3{3-4-4} sts at beginning of next 2 rows, work across: 48{54-60-66} sts.

Work even until Armholes measure approximately 2{2¹/₂-3-3¹/₂}"/5{6.5-7.5-9} cm, ending by working a **purl** row.

OPENING
Both sides of the Opening are worked at the same time, using separate yarn for **each** side.

Row 1: K 21{24-27-30}, K2 tog, K1; with second yarn, K1, SSK, knit across: 23{26-29-32} sts **each** side.

Row 2: Purl across; with second yarn, purl across.

Row 3: Knit across; with second yarn, knit across.

Repeat Rows 2 and 3 until the Back measures 4 rows less than the Front to the shoulders, ending by working a **purl** row.

NECK SHAPING
Maintain established pattern throughout.

Rows 1 and 2: Work across; with second yarn, bind off 7{8-9-10} sts, work across: 16{18-20-22} sts **each** side.

Work even for 2 rows.

Place sts from each shoulder onto st holders for 3-Needle Bind Off.

Instructions continued on page 36.

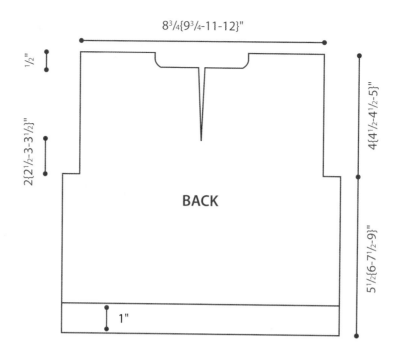

8³/₄{9³/₄-11-12}"

½"

2{2½-3-3½}"

4{4½-4½-5}"

BACK

5½{6-7½-9}"

1"

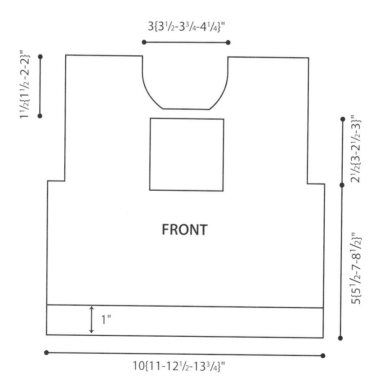

3{3½-3¾-4¼}"

1½{1½-2-2}"

2½{3-2½-3}"

FRONT

5{5½-7-8½}"

1"

10{11-12½-13¾}"

Note: Sweater includes two edge stitches.

SLEEVE (Make 2)

With straight knitting needles and Green, cast on 40{44-48-56} sts.

Row 1 (Right side): Knit across.

Row 2: Purl across.

Rows 3 and 4: Repeat Rows 1 and 2.

Row 5 (Picot row): K2, ★ YO, K2 tog; repeat from ★ across.

Repeat Rows 1 and 2 until Sleeve measures approximately 2¹⁄₂{3-3¹⁄₂-4}"/6.5{7.5-9-10} cm from cast on edge, ending by working a **purl** row.

SLEEVE CAP

Rows 1 and 2: Bind off 3{3-4-4} sts at the beginning of the next 2 rows, work across: 34{38-40-48} sts.

Bind off remaining sts **loosely.**

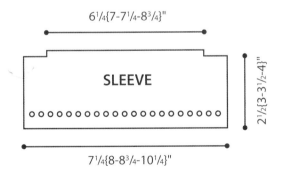

6¹⁄₄{7-7¹⁄₄-8³⁄₄}"

SLEEVE

2¹⁄₂{3-3¹⁄₂-4}"

7¹⁄₄{8-8³⁄₄-10¹⁄₄}"

FINISHING

Slip sts from Front and Back right shoulder st holders onto double-pointed knitting needles. Work 3-Needle Bind Off *(Fig. 26, page 200)*.

Repeat for left shoulder.

NECK EDGING

With circular knitting needle and corresponding colors, pick up sts evenly around Neck edge *(Figs. 22a & b, page 199)* (do **not** pick up sts along Opening).

Row 1 (Wrong side): Add on 3 sts, K1, YO (buttonhole), K2 tog, knit across.

Bind off all sts **loosely** in knit.

Sew on button opposite buttonhole.

Sew Sleeves to pullover, matching bound off stitches.

Weave underarm and side in one continuous seam *(Fig. 23, page 199)*.

Fold edge of Sleeve to **wrong** side along Picot row and sew in place. Repeat on second Sleeve.

Designed by Lisa Ellis.

boats for cameron

In Debbie's first Blossom Street book, The Shop on Blossom Street, *four women begin knitting lessons at a local yarn shop, never realizing they will soon be knitting baby gifts for one of their classmates.*

Cables can be fun to make, because all it takes is a neat little trick to form a fabric that almost looks braided. Since the Panel is only twelve stitches wide, you can practice making the cables and see fast results.

◼◼◼◻ **INTERMEDIATE**

Finished Size: 36" x 44" (91.5 cm x 112 cm)

MATERIALS

Bulky Weight Yarn **5**
[4 ounces, 155 yards
(113 grams, 140 meters) per skein]:
   Blue - 5 skeins
   White - 2 skeins
Straight knitting needles **and** 29" (73.5 cm)
   Circular knitting needle for Borders,
   size 11 (8 mm) **or** size needed for gauge
Cable needle
Stitch holders - 5
Yarn needle

GAUGE: In Stockinette Stitch,
       12 sts and 16 rows = 4" (10 cm)

Technique used:
• YO (*Fig. 5a, page 194*)

CABLE PANEL (Make 2)

With White and straight needles, cast on 12 sts.

Row 1: P1, K2, P6, K2, P1.

Row 2 (Right side): K1, P2, K6, P2, K1.

Row 3: P1, K2, P6, K2, P1.

Row 4: K1, P2, slip next 3 sts onto cable needle and hold in **back** of work, K3 from left needle, K3 from cable needle, P2, K1.

Rows 5-11: Repeat Rows 1 and 2, 3 times; then repeat Row 1 once **more**.

Rows 12-151: Repeat Rows 4-11, 17 times; then repeat Rows 4-7 once **more**.

Slip stitches onto stitch holder.

Instructions continued on page 40.

BOAT PANEL (Make 3)

With Blue and straight needles, cast on 24 sts.

Row 1: Purl across.

Row 2 (Right side)**:** Knit across.

Rows 3-7: Repeat Rows 1 and 2 twice, then repeat Row 1 once **more**.

Row 8: K7, P 10, K7.

Row 9: P6, K 12, P6.

Row 10: K5, P 14, K5.

Row 11: Purl across.

Row 12: Knit across.

Row 13: P4, K6, P1, K9, P4.

Row 14: K5, P8, K1, P6, K4.

Row 15: P4, K6, P1, K8, P5.

Row 16: K6, P7, K1, P5, K5.

Row 17: P5, K5, P1, K6, P7.

Row 18: K7, P6, K1, P4, K6.

Row 19: P6, K4, P1, K5, P8.

Row 20: K9, P4, K1, P3, K7.

Row 21: P7, K3, P1, K4, P9.

Row 22: K 10, P3, K1, P2, K8.

Row 23: P8, K2, P1, K2, P 11.

Row 24: K 11, P2, K1, P1, K9.

Row 25: P 11, K1, P 12.

Row 26: Knit across.

Row 27: Purl across.

Rows 28-37: Repeat Rows 26 and 27, 5 times.

Rows 38-151: Repeat Rows 8-37, 3 times; then repeat Rows 8-31 once **more**.

Slip stitches onto stitch holder.

ASSEMBLY

Using photo as a guide for placement and alternating Panels, whipstitch Panels together (**Fig. 24, page 199**).

TOP BORDER

The Border is worked separately across each side of the Blanket, using a yarn over to increase stitches and form a pattern. The Border is then sewn together at the corners.

With **right** side facing, slip sts from st holders onto circular needle: 96 sts.

Row 1: With Blue, knit across.

Row 2: Purl across.

Row 3: K1, YO, knit across to last st, YO, K1.

Row 4: Knit across.

Rows 5-7: Repeat Rows 3 and 4 once, then repeat Row 3 once **more**.

Rows 8-18: Repeat Rows 2-7 once, then repeat Rows 2-6 once **more**.

Bind off all sts in **knit**.

BOTTOM BORDER

Tip: When stitches are picked up and knit one at a time, it prevents a ridge from forming on the wrong side, as it would if the stitches are only picked up and not knit until the next row.

To pick up and knit stitches, pick up a stitch *(Figs. 22a & b, page 199)* and place it on the left needle, then knit the stitch.

With **right** side facing, using circular needle and Blue, pick up and knit 24 sts across each Boat Panel and 12 sts across each Cable Panel across bottom edge: 96 sts.

Work same as Top Border Rows 2-18.

SIDE BORDER (Make 2)

With **right** side facing, using circular needle and Blue, pick up and knit evenly across long edge.

Work same as Top Border Rows 2-18.

Sew corners together.

Weave in all yarn ends.

Design by Bonita Dubil.

baby blocks

This is the original blanket by designer Ann Norling that appeared in Debbie's book, The Shop on Blossom Street. It is the design that the character Lydia Hoffman chooses for her beginners' knitting class. As Lydia says, the knit and purl stitches make the pattern challenging enough to keep it interesting, yet not so difficult that it would discourage a beginner.

◨◼▢▢▢ **EASY**

Finished Size: 34" x 45" (86.5 cm x 114.5 cm)

MATERIALS
Medium Weight Yarn **MEDIUM 4**
[3.5 ounces, 166 yards
(100 grams, 152 meters) per skein]: 8 skeins
29" (73.5 cm) or 36" (91.5 cm) Circular
knitting needle, size 8 (5 mm) **or** size
needed for gauge
Yarn needle

GAUGE: In pattern,
20 sts = 4" (10 cm)

Gauge Swatch: 4¹/₄" (10.75 cm) wide
Cast on 21 sts.
Work same as Bottom Border.
Bind off all sts in pattern.

A row counter may be handy to keep track of which pattern row you're on.

BOTTOM BORDER

Cast on 171 sts.

Row 1: K3, (P3, K3) across.

Row 2: P3, (K3, P3) across.

Row 3: K3, (P3, K3) across.

Rows 4 and 5: P3, (K3, P3) across.

Row 6: K3, (P3, K3) across.

Row 7: P3, (K3, P3) across.

Rows 8 and 9: K3, (P3, K3) across.

Row 10: P3, (K3, P3) across.

Row 11: K3, (P3, K3) across.

Row 12: P3, (K3, P3) across.

Instructions continued on page 44.

BODY

Row 1: P3, K3, P3, K9, (P9, K9) across to last 9 sts, P3, K3, P3.

Row 2: K3, P3, K3, P9, (K9, P9) across to last 9 sts, K3, P3, K3.

Rows 3 and 4: Repeat Rows 1 and 2.

Row 5: K3, P3, K 12, P9, (K9, P9) across to last 18 sts, K 12, P3, K3.

Row 6: P3, K3, P 12, K9, (P9, K9) across to last 18 sts, P 12, K3, P3.

Rows 7 and 8: Repeat Rows 5 and 6.

Rows 9-11: Repeat Rows 1 and 2 once, then repeat Row 1 once **more**.

Rows 12 and 13: Repeat Row 2.

Rows 14-16: Repeat Rows 1 and 2 once, then repeat Row 1 once **more**.

Row 17: Repeat Row 6.

Rows 18-20: Repeat Rows 5 and 6 once, then repeat Row 5 once **more**.

Row 21: Repeat Row 2.

Rows 22-24: Repeat Rows 1 and 2 once, then repeat Row 1 once **more**.

Repeat Rows 1-24 for pattern until Blanket measures approximately 42" (106.5 cm) from cast on edge, ending by working **Row 12**.

TOP BORDER

Repeat Rows 1-12 of Bottom Border.

Bind off all sts in pattern.

Weave in all yarn ends.

Design by Ann Norling.

a lesson on color

Another gorgeous baby blanket inspired by The Shop on Blossom Street, *this textured pattern is fairly easy to knit and has a simple yet colorful border that echoes all the hues in the body of the blanket.*

Shown on page 47.

■■■□ INTERMEDIATE

Using the same decrease for each row causes the yarn over pattern to slant in the same direction as the decrease. The SSK slants to the left and the K2 together slants to the right. Alternating lace blocks made of opposite decreases will form a natural ripple on all of the edges. A crocheted edging is added for extra emphasis.

Finished Size: 33" (84 cm) square

MATERIALS

Fine Weight Yarn
[2.5 ounces, 168 yards
(70 grams, 154 meters) per skein]:
    Purple - 2 skeins
    Lime - 2 skeins
    Turquoise - 2 skeins
    Coral - 2 skeins
29" (73.5 cm) or 36" (91.5 cm) Circular
    knitting needle, size 4 (3.5 mm) **or** size
    needed for gauge
Crochet hook for Edging, size E (3.5 mm)
Tapestry needle

GAUGE: In pattern,
    2 repeats (32 sts) = 5¼" (13.25 cm);
    36 rows = 4" (10 cm)

Gauge Swatch: 6"w x 4"h (15.25 cm x 10 cm)
With Purple, cast on 37 sts.
Work same as Blanket for 36 rows.
Bind off all sts in knit.

Techniques used:
• YO *(Fig. 5a, page 194)*
• K2 tog *(Fig. 11, page 196)*
• SSK *(Figs. 13a-c, page 196)*
• basic crochet sts *(page 203)*

Instructions continued on page 46.

BLANKET

With Purple, cast on 197 sts.

Rows 1 and 2: Knit across.

Row 3 (Right side): K2, (SSK, YO) 4 times, ★ K8, (SSK, YO) 4 times; repeat from ★ across to last 11 sts, K 11.

Row 4: Purl across.

Rows 5-10: Repeat Rows 3 and 4, 3 times.

Row 11: K 11, (YO, K2 tog) 4 times, ★ K8, (YO, K2 tog) 4 times; repeat from ★ across to last 2 sts, K2.

Row 12: Purl across.

Rows 13-18: Repeat Rows 11 and 12, 3 times.

Rows 19-34: Repeat Rows 3-18.

Rows 35 and 36: Knit across.

Repeat Rows 1-36 for pattern working 36 rows with each color in the following color sequence: Lime, Turquoise, Coral, Purple, Lime, Turquoise, Coral.

Bind off all sts in knit.

BORDER

Rnd 1: With **right** side facing, join Purple with sc in any corner; sc evenly around entire blanket working 2 sc in each peak, skipping one st at each dip, and working 3 sc in each corner; join with slip st to first sc, finish off.

Rnds 2-4: Repeat Rnd 1 working in the following color sequence: Lime, Turquoise, Coral.

Weave in all yarn ends.

Design by Deborah Robson.

welcome, little onesie

In Back on Blossom Street, *the women of Lydia's knitting class are experiencing many changes in their lives. And rumor has it, someone may be having a baby! The cable design on the bodice of this onesie is extra-sweet, while the dotted yarn makes the whole garment seem like a celebration.*

■■■□ INTERMEDIATE

Size	Finished Chest Measurement
3 months	18" (45.5 cm)
6 months	20" (51 cm)
12 months	21" (53.5 cm)
18 months	22" (56 cm)

Size Note: Instructions are written for size 3 months, with sizes 6, 12, and 18 months in braces { }. Instructions will be easier to read if you circle all the numbers pertaining to your infant's size. If only one number is given, it applies to all sizes.

MATERIALS
Double Knitting Weight Yarn

[1³/₄ ounces, 186 yards
(50 grams, 170 meters) per skein]:
    Spot Print - 3{3-4-4} skeins
    Peach, Mint, Yellow and Blue -
        1{1-2-2} skeins **each** color
16" (40.5 cm) **or** 24" (61 cm) Circular knitting
    needle, size 5 (3.75 mm) **or** size needed
    for gauge
Straight knitting needles, size 3 (3.25 mm)
Cable needle
Stitch holders - 3
Markers
¹/₂" (12 mm) Buttons - 3
Snap tape - 12{14-16-18}"/
    30.5{35.5-40.5-45.5} cm length
Yarn needle
Sewing needle and matching thread

GAUGE: With circular knitting needle,
in Stockinette Stitch,
24 sts and 32 rows = 4" (10 cm)

Techniques used:
• YO *(Fig. 5a, page 194)*
• adding new sts *(Figs. 6a & b, page 195)*
• increasing evenly *(page 195)*
• knit increase *(Figs. 7a & b, page 195)*
• K2 tog *(Fig. 11, page 196)*
• SSK *(Figs. 13a-c, page 196)*

STITCH GUIDE

CABLE 2 BACK *(abbreviated C2B)*
Slip next 2 sts onto cable needle and hold in **back** of work, K2 from left needle, K2 from cable needle.

CABLE 2 FRONT *(abbreviated C2F)*
Slip next 2 sts onto cable needle and hold in **front** of work, K2 from left needle, K2 from cable needle.

FIRST LEG
RIBBING
With Blue and straight knitting needles, cast on 38{40-40-42} sts **loosely**.

Work in K1, P1 ribbing for 1¹/₂" (4 cm) increasing 4{6-4-2} sts evenly spaced across last row: 42{46-44-44} sts.

Instructions continued on page 50.

BODY
Change to circular knitting needle.

Row 1 (Right side)**:** With Spot Print, knit across.

Row 2: Purl across.

Rows 3 and 4: Repeat Rows 1 and 2.

Row 5: Increase in first st, knit across to last 2 sts, increase in next st, K1: 44{48-46-46} sts.

Working in Stockinette Stitch, continue to increase in same manner, every fourth row, 0{2-4-6} times **more** *(see Zeros, page 191)*; then increase every sixth row, 4 times: 52{60-62-66} sts.

Work even until piece measures approximately 5^1/$_2${6^1/$_2$-7^1/$_2$-8^1/$_2$}"/14{16.5-19-21.5} cm from cast on edge, ending by working a **purl** row.

SHAPING
Row 1 (Increase row)**:** Increase in first st, knit across: 53{61-63-67} sts.

Row 2: Purl across.

Rows 3 and 4: Repeat Rows 1 and 2: 54{62-64-68} sts.

Row 5: Add on 7{6-7-7} sts **loosely**: 61{68-71-75} sts.

Slip sts onto a st holder.

SECOND LEG
Work same as First Leg to Shaping: 52{60-62-66} sts.

SHAPING
Row 1 (Increase row)**:** Knit across to last 2 sts, increase in next st, K1: 53{61-63-67} sts.

Row 2: Purl across.

Rows 3 and 4: Repeat Rows 1 and 2: 54{62-64-68} sts.

Row 5: Increase in first st, knit across; slip sts from the First Leg st holder onto the opposite end of the circular knitting needle, knit across to last 2 sts, increase in next st, K1: 117{132-137-145} sts.

Row 6: Purl across.

Row 7: Increase in first st, knit across to last 2 sts, increase in next st, K1: 119{134-139-147} sts.

Row 8: Purl across; cut yarn.

BODY
With **right** side facing, slip first 56{64-66-70} sts to opposite end of circular knitting needle, place a marker to mark the beginning of the round *(see Markers, page 191)*, with Spot Print knit across remaining 63{70-73-77} sts, **turn;** add on 7{6-7-7} sts, **turn;** knit around to marker: 126{140-146-154} sts.

Knit every round until Body measures approximately 7{8^3/$_4$-10^1/$_2$-12^1/$_4$}"/18{22-26.5-31} cm from last added on sts.

Next Rnd: K3{3-4-3}, K2 tog, ★ K5{5-6-5}, K2 tog; repeat from ★ around to last 2{2-4-2} sts, K2{2-4-2}: 108{120-128-132} sts.

Next Rnd: Purl around.

Next Rnd: Knit around.

Next Rnd (Garter ridge): Purl around.

LEFT BACK YOKE

Row 1: Bind off 6 sts, K9, with Peach K8, with Spot Print K6{9-11-12}, slip next 54{60-64-66} sts onto first st holder for Front, slip remaining 24{27-29-30} sts onto second st holder for Right Back Yoke: 24{27-29-30} sts.

Row 2: P5{8-10-11}, K1, with Peach P8, with Spot Print K1, purl across.

Row 3: K 10, with Peach C2B, C2F, with Spot Print knit across.

Row 4: P5{8-10-11}, K1, with Peach P8, with Spot Print K1, purl across.

Row 5: K 10, with Peach K8, with Spot knit across.

Rows 6-8: Repeat Rows 4 and 5 once, then repeat Row 4 once **more**.

Repeat Rows 3-8 until Left Back Yoke measures approximately 3¹/₄{3¹/₂-3³/₄-4}"/8.5{9-9.5-10} cm from Garter ridge, ending by working a **wrong** side row.

NECK SHAPING

Row 1: K5{7-7-7}, slip sts just worked onto a st holder, work across: 19{20-22-23} sts.

Row 2: Work across.

Row 3: SSK, work across: 18{19-21-22} sts.

Row 4: Work across.

Bind off remaining sts in pattern.

FRONT YOKE

With **right** side facing, slip 54{60-64-66} sts from Front st holder onto circular knitting needle.

Row 1: With Spot Print K6{9-11-12}, with Peach K8, with Spot Print K9, with Mint K8, with Spot Print K9, with Yellow K8, with Spot Print knit across.

Row 2: P5{8-10-11}, K1, with Yellow P8, with Spot Print K1, P7, K1, with Mint P8, with Spot Print, K1, P7, K1, with Peach P8, with Spot Print K1, purl across.

Row 3: K6{9-11-12}, with Peach C2B, C2F, with Spot Print K9, with Mint C2B, C2F, with Spot Print K9, with Yellow C2B, C2F, with Spot Print knit across.

Row 4: P5{8-10-11}, K1, with Yellow P8, with Spot Print K1, P7, K1, with Mint P8, with Spot Print, K1, P7, K1, with Peach P8, with Spot Print K1, purl across.

Rows 5-8: Repeat Rows 1 and 2 twice.

Instructions continued on page 52.

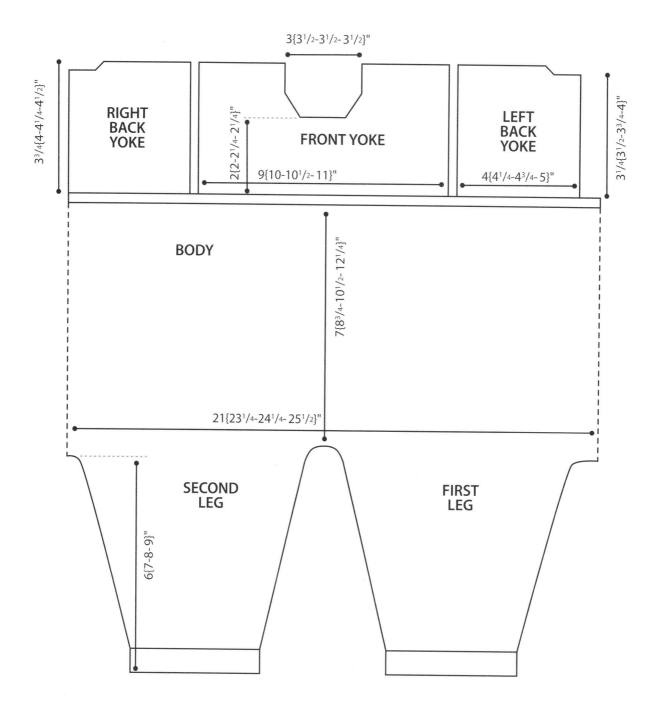

3{3½-3½- 3½}"

RIGHT BACK YOKE

FRONT YOKE

LEFT BACK YOKE

3³/4{4-4¹/4-4¹/2}"

3¹/4{3¹/2-3³/4-4}"

2{2-2¹/4- 2¹/4}"

9{10-10¹/2- 11}"

4{4¹/4-4³/4- 5}"

BODY

7{8³/4-10¹/2- 12¹/4}"

21{23¹/4-24¹/4- 25¹/2}"

SECOND LEG

FIRST LEG

6{7-8-9}"

Note: Dashed lines indicate continuous rounds.

Repeat Rows 3-8 until Front Yoke measures approximately 2{2-2$\frac{1}{4}$-2$\frac{1}{4}$}"/5{5-5.5-5.5} cm from Garter ridge, ending by working a **wrong** side row.

NECK SHAPING
Both sides of Neck are worked at the same time, using separate yarns for **each** side.

Row 1 (Right side): Work across 21{22-24-25} sts, slip next 12{16-16-16} sts onto a st holder; with separate yarns, work across: 21{22-24-25} sts **each** side.

Row 2: Work across; with separate yarns, work across.

Row 3 (Decrease row): Work across to within 2 sts of Neck edge, K2 tog; with separate yarns, SSK, work across: 20{21-23-24} sts **each** side.

Rows 4-7: Repeat Rows 2 and 3 twice: 18{19-21-22} sts **each** side.

Work even until Front Yoke measures same as Left Back Yoke, ending by working a **wrong** side row.

Bind off remaining sts in pattern.

RIGHT BACK YOKE
With **right** side facing, slip sts from Right Back Yoke st holder onto circular knitting needle: 24{27-29-30} sts.

Row 1 (Right side): With Spot Print K6{9-11-12}, with Yellow K8, with Spot Print knit across.

Row 2: P9, K1, with Yellow P8, with Spot Print K1, purl across.

Row 3: K6{9-11-12}, with Yellow C2B, C2F, with Spot Print knit across.

Row 4: P9, K1, with Yellow P8, with Spot Print K1, purl across.

Rows 5-8: Repeat Rows 1 and 2 twice.

Repeat Rows 3-8 until Right Back Yoke measures 3$\frac{1}{4}${3$\frac{1}{2}$-3$\frac{3}{4}$-4}"/8.5{9-9.5-10} cm from Garter ridge, ending by working a **right** side row.

NECK SHAPING
Row 1: P5{7-7-7} sts, slip sts just worked onto a st holder, work across: 19{20-22-23} sts.

Row 2: Work across to last 2 sts, K2 tog: 18{19-21-22} sts.

Rows 3 and 4: Work across.

Bind off remaining sts in pattern.

LEFT SLEEVE
RIBBING
With Yellow and straight knitting needles, cast on 30{32-34-36} sts **loosely**.

Work in K1, P1 ribbing for 1$\frac{1}{2}$" (4 cm) increasing 16{16-18-18} sts evenly spaced across last row: 46{48-52-54} sts.

Instructions continued on page 54.

BODY
Change to circular knitting needles.

With Spot Print, work in Stockinette Stitch until Left Sleeve measures approximately 5{6-7-9}"/ 12.5{15-18-23} cm from cast on edge, ending by working a **purl** row.

Bind off all sts **loosely**.

RIGHT SLEEVE
RIBBING
With Peach and straight knitting needles, cast on 30{32-34-36} sts **loosely**.

Work in K1, P1 ribbing for 1½" (4 cm) increasing 16{16-18-18} sts evenly spaced across last row: 46{48-52-54} sts.

BODY
Change to circular knitting needle.

With Spot Print, work in Stockinette Stitch until Right Sleeve measures approximately 5{6-7-9}"/12.5{15-18-23} cm from cast on edge, ending by working a **purl** row.

Bind off all sts **loosely**.

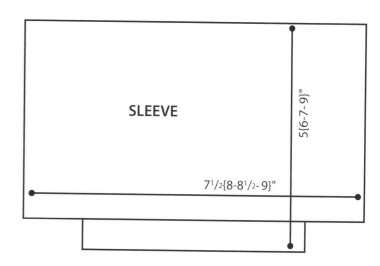

SLEEVE

5{6-7-9}"

7½{8-8½-9}"

FINISHING
Sew shoulder seams.
Weave Sleeve seams (*Fig. 23, page 199*).
Set Sleeves into armhole and sew in place.

LEFT BACK YOKE RIBBING
With **right** side facing, using straight knitting needles and Mint, pick up 20{22-24-26} sts evenly spaced across Yoke edge (*Figs. 22a & b, page 199*).

Rows 1-7: (K1, P1) across.

Bind off all sts in ribbing.

RIGHT BACK YOKE RIBBING

With **right** side facing, using straight knitting needles and Mint, pick up 20{22-24-26} sts evenly spaced across Yoke edge.

Rows 1-3: (K1, P1) across.

Row 4 (Buttonhole row): Work across 6{8-8-8} sts, ★ K2 tog, YO, work across next 5{5-6-7} sts; repeat from ★ once **more**.

Rows 5-7: (K1, P1) across.

Bind off all sts in ribbing.

NECK RIBBING

With **right** side facing, using straight knitting needles and Blue, pick up 6 sts along edge of Left Back Yoke Ribbing, K5{7-7-7} sts from st holder, pick up 12{13-13-13} sts along left neck edge, slip 12{16-16-16} sts from Front st holder onto empty knitting needle and knit across, pick up 13{14-14-14} sts along right neck edge, slip 5{7-7-7} sts from st holder onto empty knitting needle and knit across, pick up 6 sts along Right Back Yoke Ribbing: 59{69-69-69} sts.

Row 1: P1, (K1, P1) across.

Row 2: K1, (P1, K1) across.

Row 3: P1, (K1, P1) across.

Row 4 (Buttonhole row): K1, (P1, K1) across to last 4 sts, YO, K2 tog, P1, K1.

Rows 5-7: Repeat Rows 1-3.

Bind off all sts **loosely** in ribbing.

FRONT INNER LEG RIBBING

With **right** side facing, using straight knitting needles and Mint, pick up 87{101-113-127} sts evenly spaced across inner leg edge of Front.

Row 1: P1, (K1, P1) across.

Row 2: K1, (P1, K1) across.

Rows 3-7: Repeat Rows 1 and 2 twice, then repeat Row 1 once **more**.

Bind off all sts in ribbing.

BACK INNER LEG RIBBING

With **right** side facing, using straight knitting needles and Yellow, pick up 87{101-113-127} sts evenly spaced across inner leg edge of Back.

Complete same as Front Inner Leg Ribbing.

Sew female side of snap tape to **wrong** side of Front Inner Leg Ribbing; sew male side of snap tape to **right** side of Back Inner Leg Ribbing.
Sew edge of Yoke ribbing to bound off sts at base of Yoke.
Sew buttons to Left Back Yoke Ribbing opposite buttonholes.

Designed by Joan Beebe.

baby bonnet

In Hannah's List, there are several knitters who are using this little bonnet pattern for a future arrival. The new baby will have plenty of hats to go with all of his/her outfits.

◼◼◻◻ **EASY +**

Finished Size: 6 months

MATERIALS

Light Weight Yarn 🧶 **LIGHT 3**
[1.75 ounces, 161 yards
(50 grams, 147 meters) per skein]:
   1 skein
Straight knitting needles, sizes 5 (3.75 mm)
   and 6 (4 mm) **or** sizes needed for gauge
Cable needle
Tapestry needle
Sewing needle and thread
⅝" (16 mm) Button

Techniques used:

• YO (*Fig. 5a, page 194*)
• adding new stitches (*Figs. 6a & b, page 195*)
• K2 tog (*Fig. 11, page 196*)

GAUGE: With larger size needles,
   in pattern, 22 sts and
   38 rows = 3¾" (9.5 cm)

Gauge Swatch: 3¾" (9.5 cm) square
Using larger size needles, cast on 22 sts.
Row 1: Knit across.
Row 2: K3, P4, K7, P4, K4.
Row 3: K4, work Back Cable, K7, work Back Cable, K3.
Row 4: K3, P4, K7, P4, K4.
Rows 5-38: Repeat Rows 1-4, 8 times; then repeat Rows 1 and 2 once **more**.
Bind off all sts in **knit**.

STITCH GUIDE

BACK CABLE (uses 4 sts)
Slip next 2 sts onto cable needle and hold in **back** of work, K2 from left needle, K2 from cable needle.

CROWN
RIBBING

Using smaller size needles, cast on 75 sts.

Row 1: K1, (P1, K1) across.

Row 2 (Right side): P1, (K1, P1) across.

Repeat Rows 1 and 2 until Ribbing measures approximately 1" (2.5 cm) from cast on edge, ending by working Row 1.

Instructions continued on page 58.

BODY

Change to larger size needles.

Row 1: Knit across.

Row 2: K8, P4, (K7, P4) across to last 8 sts, K8.

Row 3: K8, work Back Cable, (K7, work Back Cable) across to last 8 sts, K8.

Row 4: K8, P4, (K7, P4) across to last 8 sts, K8.

Repeat Rows 1-4 for pattern until Crown measures approximately 5" (12.5 cm) from cast on edge, ending by working Row 4.

BACK

Maintain established pattern throughout.

Rows 1 and 2: Bind off 25 sts, work across: 25 sts.

Work even until Back measures approximately 4" (10 cm) from bound off sts, ending by working pattern Row 4.

Bind off all sts in **knit**.

FINISHING

Sew sides of Back to bound off edges of Crown.

NECK RIBBING

With **right** side facing and using smaller size needles, pick up 81 sts across bottom edge *(Figs. 22a & b, page 199)*, **turn**; add on 20 sts: 101 sts.

Row 1: P1, (K1, P1) across.

Row 2: K1, (P1, K1) across.

Row 3: P1, (K1, P1) across.

Row 4: K1, (P1, K1) across.

Row 5 (Buttonhole row): P1, K2 tog, YO, (K1, P1) across.

Rows 6-9: Repeat Rows 2 and 3 twice.

Bind off all sts **loosely** in ribbing.

Sew button on left side of Neck Ribbing.

Design by Lois J. Long.

baby's hooded cardigan

This is another pattern that's proving popular with Lydia's customers in Back on Blossom Street. It uses six additional colors to give the white cardigan the look having been dipped in a pastel rainbow. Such a sweet design!

Shown on page 61.

■■■□ INTERMEDIATE

Size	Finished Chest Measurement
6 months	22" (56 cm)
12 months	23" (59.5 cm)
18 months	25" (63.5 cm)

Size Note: Instructions are written for size 6 months, with sizes 12 & 18 months in braces { }. Instructions will be easier to read if you circle all the numbers pertaining to your infant's size. If only one number is given, it applies to all sizes.

MATERIALS

Light Weight Yarn LIGHT 3
[1³/₄ ounces, 186 yards
(50 grams, 170 meters) per skein]:
    White - 3{4-5} skeins
    6 Contrasting Colors - 1 skein **each** color
        (we used Baby Blue, Pale Yellow, Peach,
        Lt Green, Lavender, and Baby Pink)
Straight knitting needles, sizes 4 (3.5 mm)
   and 6 (4 mm) **or** sizes needed for gauge
Stitch holders - 2
¹/₂" (12 mm) Buttons - 6{6-8}
Yarn needle

GAUGE: With larger size needles,
      in Body pattern,
      23 sts and 32 rows = 4" (10 cm)

Techniques used:
• YO (*Figs. 5a & d, page 194*)
• increasing evenly (*page 195*)
• knit increase (*Figs. 7a & b, page 195*)
• K2 tog (*Fig. 11, page 196*)
• slip 1, K1, PSSO (*Figs. 14a & b, page 197*)
• slip 1, K2 tog, PSSO (*Fig. 16, page 197*)
• P3 tog (*Fig. 20, page 198*)

Cardigan is worked in one piece to underarm.

CARDIGAN
RIBBING
With White and smaller size needles,
cast on 115{121-133} sts **loosely**.

Row 1: P2, K1, (P1, K1) across to last 2 sts, P2.

Row 2 (Right side): K2, P1, (K1, P1) across to last 2 sts, K2.

Instructions continued on page 60.

Rows 3-10: Repeat Rows 1 and 2, 4 times.

Row 11: Work across increasing 8{10-10} sts evenly spaced across: 123{131-143} sts.

BODY
Change to larger size needles.

Rows 1-4: Beginning with a **knit** row, work in Stockinette Stitch (knit one row, purl one row) for 4 rows.

When instructed to slip a stitch, always slip as if to **purl** unless instructed otherwise. Carry yarn **loosely** along the **wrong** side of the work when slipping stitches.

Row 5: Slip 3{1-5}, with next new color K5{3-5}, (slip 3, K5) across to last 3{7-5} sts, (slip 3, K3) 0{1-0} time(s) *(see Zeros, page 191)*, leave remaining 3{1-5} st(s) unworked; **turn**.

Row 6: K5{3-5}, (slip 3, K5) across to last 3{7-5} sts, (slip 3, K3) 0{1-0} time(s), slip last 3{1-5} sts; cut new color.

Rows 7-12: With White, work in Stockinette Stitch for 6 rows.

Row 13: Slip 1{3-1}, with next new color K3{5-5}, slip 3, (K5, slip 3) across to last 4{8-6} sts, K3{5-5}, leave remaining 1{3-1} st(s) unworked; **turn**.

Row 14: K3(5-5}, slip 3, (K5, slip 3) across to last 4{8-6} sts, K3{5-5}, slip 1{3-1}; cut new color.

Rows 15-20: With White, work in Stockinette Stitch for 6 rows.

Repeat Rows 5-20 for pattern until piece measures approximately 6$\frac{1}{2}${7$\frac{1}{2}$-8$\frac{1}{2}$}"/16.5{19-21.5} cm from cast on edge, ending by working Row 6 or Row 14.

RIGHT FRONT
Row 1: With White K 29{31-34}, slip next 65{69-75} sts onto first st holder for Back, slip remaining 29{31-34} sts onto second st holder for Left Front: 29{31-34} sts.

Rows 2-4: Work in Stockinette Stitch for 3 rows.

Row 5: With next new color K2, (slip 3, K1) across to last 3{5-0} sts, slip 2{3-0}, K1{2-0}.

Row 6: P1{3-2}, (slip 1, P3) across.

Row 7: Knit across.

Row 8: Purl across.

Repeat Rows 5-8 for pattern until piece measures approximately 9$\frac{1}{2}${10$\frac{3}{4}$-12}"/24{27.5-30.5} cm from cast on edge, ending by working a **wrong** side row.

Instructions continued on page 62.

NECK SHAPING
Maintain established pattern throughout.

Row 1: Bind off 5{6-6} sts, work across: 24{25-28} sts.

Row 2: Work across.

Row 3 (Decrease row): Slip 1 as if to **knit**, K1, PSSO, work across: 23{24-27} sts.

Repeat Rows 2 and 3, 2{2-3} times: 21{22-24} sts.

Work even until Right Front measures approximately 11{12½-14}"/28{32-35.5} cm from cast on edge, ending by working a **wrong** side row.

Bind off all remaining sts.

BACK

With **right** side facing, slip 65{69-75} sts from Back st holder onto an empty larger size needle.

Rows 1-4: With White, work in Stockinette Stitch for 4 rows.
Row 5: With next new color K1{1-2}, slip 3, (K1, slip 3) across to last 1{1-2} st(s), K1{1-2}.

Row 6: P2{2-3}, slip 1, (P3, slip 1) across to last 2{2-3} sts, P2{2-3}.

Row 7: Knit across.

Row 8: Purl across.

Repeat Rows 5-8 for pattern until Back measures same as Right Front, ending by working a **wrong** side row.

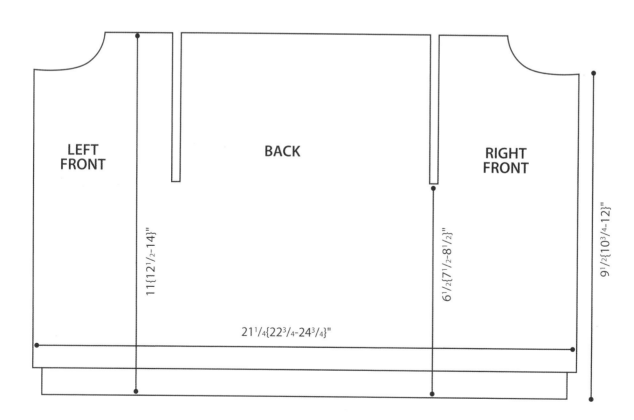

LEFT FRONT

BACK

RIGHT FRONT

11{12½-14}"

6½{7½-8½}"

9½{10¾-12}"

21¼{22¾-24¾}"

Note: Sweater includes two edge stitches.

Bind off first 21{22-24} sts, work across until there are 23{25-27} sts on the right needle, slip these 23{25-27} sts onto the st holder; bind off remaining sts.

LEFT FRONT

With **right** side facing, slip 29{31-34} sts from Left Front st holder onto an empty larger size needle.

Rows 1-4: With White, work in Stockinette Stitch for 4 rows.

Row 5: With next new color K1{2-1}, slip 2{3-3}, (K1, slip 3) across to last 2 sts, K2.

Row 6: (P3, slip 1) across to last 1{3-2} st(s), P1{3-2}.
Row 7: Knit across.

Row 8: Purl across.

Repeat Rows 5-8 until Left Front measures same as Right Front to Neck Shaping, ending by working a **right** side row.

NECK SHAPING

Row 1: Bind off 5{6-6} sts, work across: 24{25-28} sts.

Row 2 (Decrease row): Work across to last 2 sts, K2 tog: 23{24-27} sts.

Row 3: Work across.

Repeat Rows 2 and 3, 2{2-3} times: 21{22-24} sts.

Work even until Left Front measures same as Right Front, ending by working a **wrong** side row.

Bind off remaining sts.

Sew shoulder seams.

NECK RIBBING

With **right** side facing, using smaller size needles and White, and beginning **after** bound off sts, pick up 14{16-18} sts evenly spaced across Right Front neck edge (*Figs. 22a & b, page 199*), knit 23{25-27} sts from Back neck st holder, pick up 14{16-18} sts evenly spaced across Left Front neck edge (do **not** pick up sts in bound off edge): 51{57-63} sts.

Row 1: K1, (P1, K1) across.

Row 2: P1, (K1, P1) across.
Rows 3-6: Repeat Rows 1 and 2 twice.

Row 7: Work across increasing 10 sts evenly spaced: 61{67-73} sts.

HOOD
Change to larger size needles.

Rows 1-4: Work in Stockinette Stitch for 4 rows.

Row 5: Slip 4{3-2}, with next new color K5, (slip 3, K5) across to last 4{3-2} sts, leave last 4{3-2} sts unworked; **turn.**

Instructions continued on page 64.

Row 6: K5, (slip 3, K5) across to last 4{3-2} sts, slip 4{3-2}; cut new color.

Rows 7-10: With White, work in Stockinette Stitch for 4 rows.

Row 11: K 29{32-35}, increase in next st, K1, increase in next st, knit across: 63{69-75} sts.

Row 12: Purl across.

Row 13: Slip 1, with next new color K4{3-2}, slip 3, (K5, slip 3) 2{3-3} times, K6{7-6}, slip 3, K6{5-6}, slip 3, (K5, slip 3) 2{2-3} times, K4{3-2}, leave last st unworked; **turn.**

Row 14: K4{3-2}, slip 3, (K5, slip 3) 2{3-3} times, K6{7-6}, slip 3, K6{5-6}, slip 3, (K5, slip 3) 2{2-3} times, K4{3-2}, slip 1; cut new color.

Rows 15-20: With White, work in Stockinette Stitch for 6 rows.

Row 21: Slip 4{3-2}, with next new color (K5, slip 3) 3{3-4} times, K7{6-7}, slip 3, K5{6-5}, (slip 3, K5) 2{3-3} times, leave remaining 4{3-2} sts unworked; **turn.**

Row 22: (K5, slip 3) 3{3-4} times, K7{6-7}, slip 3, K5{6-5}, (slip 3, K5) 2{3-3} times, slip 4{3-2}; cut new color.

Row 23: With White K 30{33-36}, increase in next st, K1, increase in next st, knit across: 65{71-77} sts.

Rows 24-28: Work in Stockinette Stitch for 5 rows.

Row 29: Slip 1, with next new color K4{3-2}, slip 3, (K5, slip 3) 2{2-3} times, K7, slip 3, K7{5-7}, slip 3, K5{7-5}, slip 3, (K5, slip 3) 1{2-2} time(s), K4{3-2}, leave remaining st unworked; **turn.**

Row 30: K4{3-2}, slip 3, (K5, slip 3) 2{2-3} times, K7, slip 3, K7{5-7}, slip 3, K5{7-5}, slip 3, (K5, slip 3) 1{2-2} time(s), K4{3-2}, slip 1; cut new color.

Rows 31 and 32: With White, work in Stockinette Stitch for 2 rows.

Row 33: K 31{34-37}, increase in next st, K1, increase in next st, knit across: 67{73-79} sts.

Rows 34-36: Work in Stockinette Stitch for 3 rows.

Row 37: Slip 4{3-2}, with next new color (K5, slip 3) 3{3-4} times, K4, slip 3, K4{5-4}, slip 3, K5{4-5}, (slip 3, K5) 2{3-3} times, leave remaining 4{3-2} sts unworked; **turn.**

Row 38: (K5, slip 3) 3{3-4} times, K4, slip 3, K4{5-4}, slip 3, K5{4-5}, (slip 3, K5) 2{3-3} times, slip 4{3-2}; cut new color.

Rows 39-42: With White, work in Stockinette Stitch for 4 rows.

Row 43: K 32{35-38}, increase in next st, K1, increase in next st, knit across: 69{75-81} sts.

Row 44: Purl across.

Row 45: Slip 1, with next new color, K4{3-2}, slip 3, (K5, slip 3) across to last 5{4-3} sts, K4{3-2}, leave remaining st unworked; **turn**.

Row 46: K4{3-2}, slip 3, (K5, slip 3) across to last 5{4-3} sts, K4{3-2}, slip 1; cut new color.

Rows 47-52: With White, work in Stockinette Stitch for 6 rows.

Row 53: Slip 4{3-2}, with next new color K5, (slip 3, K5) across to last 4{3-2} sts, leave last 4{3-2} sts unworked; **turn**.

Row 54: K5, (slip 3, K5) across to last 4{3-2} sts, slip 4{3-2}; cut new color.

Work even until Hood measures approximately 6¹/₂{7-7¹/₂}"/16.5{18-19} cm from top of Neck Ribbing, ending by working a **wrong** side row.

SHAPING
Maintain established pattern throughout.

Row 1: Work across 33{36-39} sts, slip 1 as if to **knit**, K2 tog, PSSO, work across: 67{73-79} sts.

Row 2: Work across 32{35-38} sts, P3 tog, work across: 65{71-77} sts.

Row 3: Work across 31{34-37} sts, slip 1 as if to **knit**, K2 tog, PSSO, work across: 63{69-75} sts.

Row 4: Work across 30{33-36} sts, P3 tog, work across: 61{67-73} sts.

Bind off remaining sts.

Fold Hood in half with decreases at fold; sew seam.

HOOD RIBBING
With **right** side facing, using smaller size needles and White, pick up 91{97-103} sts evenly spaced across Neck Ribbing and Hood.

Row 1: P1, (K1, P1) across.

Row 2 (Right side): K1, (P1, K1) across.

Rows 3-15: Repeat Rows 1 and 2, 6 times; then repeat Row 1 once **more**.

Bind off all sts **loosely** in ribbing.

Fold ribbing in half to inside and sew bound off edge **loosely** in place, forming a casing.

Sew each end of Rows 8-15 to bound off edge of Neck Shaping.

Instructions continued on page 66.

To make a twisted cord, cut four 36" (91.5 cm) lengths of yarn in desired colors. Holding all four strands together, fasten one end to a stationary object **or** have another person hold it; twist until **tight**. Fold in half and let it twist upon itself, knot both ends and cut the loops on the folded end.

Weave the twisted cord through the casing.

SLEEVE (Make 2)
RIBBING

With smaller size needles and White, cast on 37{39-41} sts **loosely**.

Row 1: P2, K1, (P1, K1) across to last 2 sts, P2.

Row 2: K2, P1, (K1, P1) across to last 2 sts, K2.

Rows 3-10: Repeat Rows 1 and 2, 4 times.

Row 11: Work across increasing 6{4-6} sts evenly spaced: 43{43-47} sts.

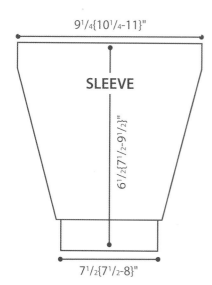

SLEEVE

9¼{10¼-11}"

6½{7½-9½}"

7½{7½-8}"

BODY
Change to larger size needles.

Row 1: With next new color, K2, slip 3, (K1, slip 3) across to last 2 sts, K2.

Row 2: P3, (slip 1, P3) across.

Row 3: Knit across.

Row 4: Purl across.

Row 5: With next new color increase in first st, K1, slip 3, (K1, slip 3) across to last 2 sts, increase in next st, K1: 45{45-49} sts.

Row 6: P4, slip 1, (P3, slip 1) across to last 4 sts, P4.

Row 7: Knit across.

Row 8: Purl across.

Row 9: With next new color increase in first st, K2, slip 3, (K1, slip 3) across to last 3 sts, K1, increase in next st, K1: 47{47-51} sts.

Row 10: P5, slip 1, (P3, slip 1) across to last 5 sts, P5.

Row 11: Knit across.

Row 12: Purl across.

Row 13: With White increase in first st, knit across to last 2 sts, increase in next st, K1: 49{49-53} sts.

Rows 14-16: Work in Stockinette Stitch for 3 rows.

Row 17: Increase in first st, knit across to last 2 sts, increase in next st, K1: 51{51-55} sts.

Row 18: Purl across.

Row 19: Slip 3{3-5}, with next new color K5, (slip 3, K5) across to last 3{3-5} sts, leave last 3{3-5} sts unworked; **turn.**

Row 20: K5, (slip 3, K5) across to last 3{3-5} sts, slip 3{3-5}; cut new color.

Rows 21 and 22: With White, work in Stockinette Stitch for 2 rows.

Row 23: Increase in first st, knit across to last 2 sts, increase in next st, K1: 53{53-57} sts.

Rows 24-26: Work in Stockinette Stitch for 3 rows.

Row 27: Slip 1{1-2}, with next new color, K4{4-5}, slip 3, (K5, slip 3) across to last 5{5-7} sts, K4{4-5}, leave last 1{1-2} st(s) unworked; **turn.**

Row 28: K4{4-5}, slip 3, (K5, slip 3) across to last 5{5-7} sts, K4{4-5}, slip 1{1-2}; cut new color.

Continue in pattern, increasing one st at each edge in same manner, every fourth row, 0{3-0} times **more**; then increase every sixth row, 0{0-3} times: 53{59-63} sts.

Work even until Sleeve measures approximately 6$\frac{1}{2}${7$\frac{1}{2}$-9$\frac{1}{2}$}"/16.5{19-24} cm from cast on edge, ending by working a **wrong** side row.

Bind off all sts **loosely**.

Weave underarm seam *(Fig. 23, page 199)*. Set Sleeve into armhole and sew in place.

(Fig. 23, page 199)

FINISHING

Work Buttonhole Band on Right Front for girls or on Left Front for boys.

BUTTONHOLE BAND

With **right** side facing, using smaller size needles and White, pick up 63{73-85} sts evenly spaced across front edge.

Row 1 (Wrong side): P1, (K1, P1) across.

Row 2: K1, (P1, K1) across.

Row 3: P1, (K1, P1) across.

Row 4 (Buttonhole row): K1, P1, K1, YO, K2 tog, ★ work across next 9{11-9} sts, YO, K2 tog; repeat from ★ across to last 3 sts, K1, P1, K1.

Rows 5-7: Repeat Rows 1-3.

Bind off all sts in ribbing.

BUTTON BAND

With **right** side facing, using smaller size needles and White, pick up 63{73-85} sts evenly spaced across front edge.

Row 1 (Wrong side): P1, (K1, P1) across.

Row 2: K1, (P1, K1) across.

Rows 3-7: Repeat Rows 1 and 2 twice, then repeat Row 1 once **more**.

Bind off all sts in ribbing.

Sew buttons to Button Band opposite buttonholes.

Designed by Joan Beebe.

In so many of Debbie's unforgettable stories, there are knitters who brighten the lives of others with their creations. These fictional characters make scarves, hats, sweaters, and shawls as caring expressions of friendship. That's because real knitters do the same thing, putting their time and talent into something uniquely wonderful for the people they love. Debbie is delighted to present this wide selection of clothing and accessories from her Knit Along pattern books. Enjoy the creativity while you cherish the special folks in your life.

garments
& accessories

felted knitting tote

In Debbie's popular Cedar Cove *book series, Charlotte Jefferson is the top collector of recipes. And if she isn't cooking something, she's knitting. This felted tote is a popular design among the knitters at the senior center where Charlotte meets her friends. The tote is so roomy, you could use it to carry enough yarn for an afghan. And maybe a notepad for jotting down recipes!*

◼◼◻◻◻ **EASY**

Finished Size: 16^1/$_2$" wide x 13^1/$_2$" high
(42 cm x 34.5 cm)

MATERIALS

Medium Weight Wool Yarn **④ MEDIUM**
[3^1/$_2$ ounces, 223 yards
(100 grams, 204 meters) per ball]:
Green - 4 balls
White - 1 ball
Pink - 1 ball
Straight knitting needles, size 10^1/$_2$ (6.5 mm)
or size needed for gauge
Yarn needle
Plastic rigid foam board for blocking

Technique used:
• adding new sts (*Figs. 6a & b, page 195*)

Felting is a lot of **fun** – when you do it on purpose! Felting is simple. You start with a large, wool-based knitted project. You put it in hot water in your washing machine. And, the project shrinks. You end up with felted knits with a strong, dense, and slightly fuzzy texture, making them perfectly **fabulous** for purses and knitting totes.

Tips for Successful Felting

Because felting is not an exact science, the results are as individual as your knitting. In choosing your yarn, first, read the label. Avoid "superwash" yarns as they are made, specifically, to NOT shrink. Choose a yarn that is at least 50% wool. Novelty yarns used as "carry along" yarn that can be washed in hot water can give great results. Just knit them as a second strand with the main yarn that does felt so they will be pulled into shape.

ALWAYS make a test swatch with all of your yarns and colors to: Check knit gauge, see how the yarn felts, make sure all the yarns in the project felt the way you want them to, and to make sure the colors do not run.

Measure your swatch BEFORE and AFTER you felt it. While this is no guarantee of the final results, it will give you an idea of how this yarn shrinks.

Hold 2 strands of yarn together throughout.

GAUGE: In Stockinette Stitch,
20 sts and 28 rows = 6" (15.25 cm)

The Body will measure 21^1/$_2$" wide x 22^1/$_2$" high (54.5 cm x 57 cm) before felting. The felting process will shrink your Tote more in the length than it does in the width.

Instructions continued on page 72.

BODY (Make 2)

With Green, cast on 71 sts.

Beginning with a **knit** row, work in Stockinette Stitch (knit one row, purl one row) for 38 rows.

Work even in the following color sequence:
3 Rows White, 2 rows **each** of Green, White, (Pink, White) twice, 8 rows Pink, 2 rows **each** of (White, Pink) 3 times, 3 rows White.

Using Green, work even for 20 rows.

Handle: K 28, bind off next 15 sts, knit across: 28 sts **each** side.

Next Row: Purl across to bound off sts; **turn**, add on 15 sts, **turn**; purl across: 71 sts.

Work even for 7 rows.

Bind off all sts in **purl**.

FINISHING
ASSEMBLY

With **wrong** sides together, whipstitch Body together along bottom edge (*Fig. 24, page 199*).
Beginning at top edge, weave Body together along one side, matching stripes and ending 2" (5 cm) from bottom edge. Bring bottom seam to meet side seam, forming a "T" shape; whipstitch this edge together. Repeat for second side.
Turn Tote right side out and tack bottom flaps in place.

Felt Tote (*see Felting, page 202*).

Design by Peggy Schultz.

cable sampler scarf

In Summer on Blossom Street, *Lydia guides her students through making a sampler scarf. This design is like getting seven different projects in one—each pattern stitch would make a lovely gift all by itself.*

Shown on page 75.

●■□□ EASY +

The Cable patterns are made up of knit and purl stitches and are formed by moving stitches to the front or back of the work allowing the stitches to switch places. Increases are used to allow for the difference in gauge of the Cable Patterns, and then decreases are used to return to the original number of stitches to work the Garter Stitch band that's between each Cable Pattern.

Finished Size: 8" x 57" (20.5 cm x 145 cm)

MATERIALS

Wool Light Weight Yarn (3 LIGHT)
[1.75 ounces, 136 yards
(50 grams, 125 meters) per hank]:
    5 hanks
Straight knitting needles, size 6 (4 mm)
    or size needed for gauge
Cable needle

Yarn Note: In order for the Scarf to block out as shown, it should be knit with a wool yarn. Synthetics have a tendency to creep back.

GAUGE: In Garter Stitch, 21 sts = 4" (10 cm)

Techniques used:
• invisible increase *(Fig. 8, page 195)*
• K2 tog *(Fig. 11, page 196)*

STITCH GUIDE

CABLE 6 BACK (uses 6 sts) *(abbreviated C6B)*
Slip next 3 sts onto cable needle and hold in **back** of work, K3 from left needle, K3 from cable needle.

CABLE 6 FRONT (uses 6 sts) *(abbreviated C6F)*
Slip next 3 sts onto cable needle and hold in **front** of work, K3 from left needle, K3 from cable needle.

CABLE 4 BACK (uses 4 sts) *(abbreviated C4B)*
Slip next 2 sts onto cable needle and hold in **back** of work, K2 from left needle, K2 from cable needle.

CABLE 4 FRONT (uses 4 sts) *(abbreviated C4F)*
Slip next 2 sts onto cable needle and hold in **front** of work, K2 from left needle, K2 from cable needle.

Instructions continued on page 74.

SCARF

Cast on 43 sts loosely.

When instructed to slip a stitch always slip as if to **purl**, with yarn held in front of work. This forms a chain selvedge for the edge of your scarf.

Bottom Band - Rows 1-10: Slip 1, knit across.

CABLE PATTERN 1

Row 1: Slip 1, K7, P3, (K3, P3) 4 times, K8.

When instructed to increase, work the invisible increase, in which you knit the stitch **below** the next stitch and then knit the next stitch.

Row 2 (Right side): Slip 1, K4, P3, (increase 3 times, P3) 5 times, K5: 58 sts.

Row 3: Slip 1, K7, P6, (K3, P6) 4 times, K8.

Row 4: Slip 1, K4, P3, (K6, P3) 5 times, K5.

Row 5: Slip 1, K7, P6, (K3, P6) 4 times, K8.

Row 6: Slip 1, K4, P3, (C6B, P3) 5 times, K5.

Row 7: Slip 1, K7, P6, (K3, P6) 4 times, K8.

Rows 8-13: Repeat Rows 4 and 5, 3 times.

Rows 14-55: Repeat Rows 6-13, 5 times; then repeat Rows 6 and 7 once **more**.

Row 56: Slip 1, K7, K2 tog 3 times, (K3, K2 tog 3 times) 4 times, K8: 43 sts.

Band - Next 10 Rows: Slip 1, knit across.

CABLE PATTERN 2

Row 1: Slip 1, K4, purl across to last 5 sts, K5.

Row 2: Slip 1, K4, P6, (K1, increase, K1, P6) 3 times, K5: 46 sts.

Row 3: Slip 1, K 10, P4, (K6, P4) twice, K 11.

Row 4: Slip 1, (K4, P6) 4 times, K5.

Instructions continued on page 76.

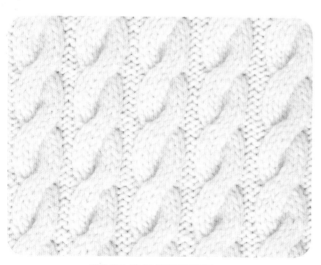

CABLE PATTERN 1

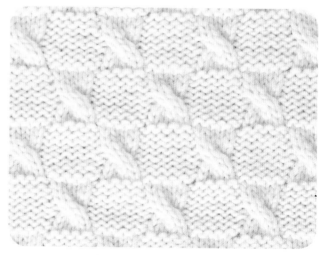

CABLE PATTERN 2

Row 5: Slip 1, K 10, P4, (K6, P4) twice, K 11.

Row 6: Slip 1, K4, P6, (C4F, P6) 3 times, K5.

Row 7: Slip 1, K 10, P4, (K6, P4) twice, K 11.

Row 8: Slip 1, (K4, P6) 4 times, K5.

Row 9: Slip 1, K 10, P4, (K6, P4) twice, K 11.

Row 10: Slip 1, K4, P1, K4, (P6, K4) 3 times, P1, K5.

Row 11: Slip 1, K5, P4, (K6, P4) 3 times, K6.

Rows 12 and 13: Repeat Rows 10 and 11.

Row 14: Slip 1, K4, P1, C4F, (P6, C4F) 3 times, P1, K5.

Row 15: Slip 1, K5, P4, (K6, P4) 3 times, K6.

Row 16: Slip 1, K4, P1, K4, (P6, K4) 3 times, P1, K5.

Row 17: Slip 1, K5, P4, (K6, P4) 3 times, K6.

Row 18: Slip 1, (K4, P6) 4 times, K5.

Rows 19-57: Repeat Rows 3-18 twice, then repeat Rows 3-9 once **more**.

Row 58: Slip 1, K 11, K2 tog, (K8, K2 tog) twice, K 12: 43 sts.

Band - Next 10 Rows: Slip 1, knit across.

CABLE PATTERN 3

Row 1: Slip 1, K7, P3, (K3, P3) 4 times, K8.

Row 2: Slip 1, K4, P3, (increase 3 times, P3) 5 times, K5: 58 sts.

Row 3: Slip 1, K7, P6, (K3, P6) 4 times, K8.

Row 4: Slip 1, K4, P3, (K6, P3) 5 times, K5.

Row 5: Slip 1, K7, P6, (K3, P6) 4 times, K8.

Row 6: Slip 1, K4, P3, (C6B, P3) 5 times, K5.

Row 7: Slip 1, K7, P6, (K3, P6) 4 times, K8.

Rows 8-13: Repeat Rows 4 and 5, 3 times.

Row 14: Slip 1, K4, P3, (C6F, P3) 5 times, K5.

Row 15: Slip 1, K7, P6, (K3, P6) 4 times, K8.

Rows 16-21: Repeat Rows 4 and 5, 3 times.

Rows 22-55: Repeat Rows 6-21 twice, then repeat Rows 6 and 7 once **more**.

Row 56: Slip 1, K7, K2 tog 3 times, (K3, K2 tog 3 times) 4 times, K8: 43 sts.

Band - Next 10 Rows: Slip 1, knit across.

CABLE PATTERN 4

Row 1 AND ALL WRONG SIDE ROWS: Slip 1, K4, purl across to last 5 sts, K5.

Row 2: Slip 1, K5, increase, K3, increase twice, (K2, increase twice) 6 times, K7: 58 sts.

Row 4: Slip 1, K4, C4F, (K2, C4F) 7 times, K7.

Row 6: Slip 1, knit across.

Row 8: Slip 1, K6, C4B, (K2, C4B) 7 times, K5.

Row 10: Slip 1, knit across.

Rows 11-57: Repeat Rows 3-10, 5 times; then repeat Rows 3-9 once **more**.

Row 58: Slip 1, K5, K2 tog, K4, K2 tog twice, (K2, K2 tog twice) 6 times, K6: 43 sts.

Band - Next 10 Rows: Slip 1, knit across.

CABLE PATTERN 5

Row 1: Slip 1, K7, P3, (K3, P3) 4 times, K8.

Row 2: Slip 1, K4, P3, (increase 3 times, P3) 5 times, K5: 58 sts.

Row 3 AND ALL WRONG SIDE ROWS: Slip 1, K7, P6, (K3, P6) 4 times, K8.

Row 4: Slip 1, K4, P3, (C4B, K2, P3) 5 times, K5.

Instructions continued on page 78.

CABLE PATTERN 3

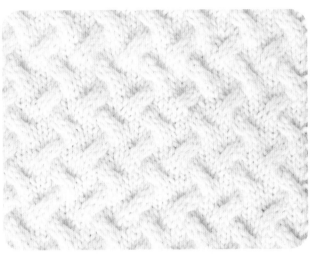

CABLE PATTERN 4

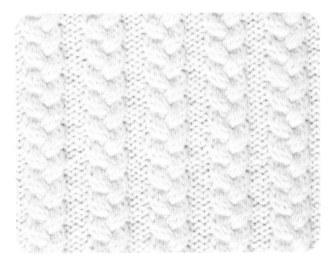

CABLE PATTERN 5

Row 6: Slip 1, K4, P3, (K2, C4F, P3) 5 times, K5.

Rows 7-55: Repeat Rows 3-6, 12 times; then repeat Row 3 once **more**.

Row 56: Slip 1, K7, K2 tog 3 times, (K3, K2 tog 3 times) 4 times, K8: 43 sts.

Band - Next 10 Rows: Slip 1, knit across.

CABLE PATTERN 6

Row 1: Slip 1, K4, purl across to last 5 sts, K5.

Row 2: Slip 1, K8, increase, K5, increase twice, (K4, increase twice) 3 times, K8: 52 sts.

Row 3 AND ALL WRONG SIDE ROWS: Slip 1, K4, purl across to last 5 sts, K5.

Row 4: Slip 1, K7, C4B, (K4, C4B) 4 times, K8.

Row 6: Slip 1, K5, C4B, C4F, (K8, C4B, C4F) twice, K6.

Row 8: Slip 1, knit across.

Row 10: Slip 1, K5, C4F, C4B, (K8, C4F, C4B) twice, K6.

Row 12: Slip 1, K7, C4B, (K4, C4B) 4 times, K8.

Row 14: Slip 1, K 13, C4B, C4F, K8, C4B, C4F, K 14.

Row 16: Slip 1, knit across.

Row 18: Slip 1, K 13, C4F, C4B, K8, C4F, C4B, K 14.

Rows 19-59: Repeat Rows 3-18 twice, then repeat Rows 3-11 once **more**.

Row 60: Slip 1, K6, K2 tog twice, ★ K5, K2 tog, K5, K2 tog twice; repeat from ★ once **more**, K9: 44 sts.

Band - Next 10 Rows: Slip 1, knit across.

CABLE PATTERN 7

Row 1: Slip 1, K7, P4, (K3, P2, K3, P4) twice, K8.

Row 2: Slip 1, K4, P3, increase 4 times, P3, ★ increase twice, P3, increase 4 times, P3; repeat from ★ once **more**, K5: 60 sts.

Row 3 AND ALL WRONG SIDE ROWS: Slip 1, K7, P8, (K3, P4, K3, P8) twice, K8.

Row 4: Slip 1, K4, P3, C4F, C4B, (P3, C4F) twice, (C4B, P3) twice, C4F, C4B, P3, K5.

Row 6: Slip 1, (K4, P3, K8, P3) 3 times, K5.

Row 8: Slip 1, K4, P3, C4B, (C4F, P3) twice, C4B, C4F, (P3, C4B) twice, C4F, P3, K5.

Row 10: Slip 1, (K4, P3, K8, P3) 3 times, K5.

Row 12: Slip 1, K4, P3, C4B, (C4F, P3) twice, C4B, C4F, (P3, C4B) twice, C4F, P3, K5.

Row 14: Slip 1, (K4, P3, K8, P3) 3 times, K5.

Row 16: Slip 1, K4, P3, C4F, C4B, (P3, C4F) twice, (C4B, P3) twice, C4F, C4B, P3, K5.

Row 18: Slip 1, (K4, P3, K8, P3) 3 times, K5.

Rows 19-57: Repeat Rows 3-18 twice, then repeat Rows 3-9 once **more**.

Row 58: Slip 1, K4, K2 tog, K1, K2 tog 4 times, ★ K3, K2 tog twice, K3, K2 tog 4 times; repeat from ★ once **more**, K8: 43 sts.

Top Band - Last 10 Rows: Slip 1, knit across.

Bind off all sts loosely in **knit**.

Design by Bev Galeskas
Fiber Trends Inc.
www.fibertrends.com

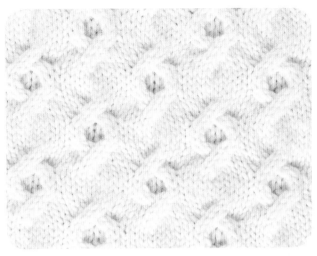

CABLE PATTERN 6

CABLE PATTERN 7

franco's muffler

Need a gift that's fairly quick to make? This easy scarf is just what you're looking for! Debbie's friend Sandy Payne designed it for her cousin Franco. Isn't he lucky to have a cousin like Sandy? It's one of 11 thoughtful designs in Debbie's Favorites.

▰▰▱▱ **EASY**

Finished Size: 6¹/₂" x 56" (16.5 cm x 142 cm)

MATERIALS

Bulky Weight Yarn **⑤**
[3¹/₂ ounces, 108 yards
(100 grams, 99 meters) per hank]:
5 hanks
Straight knitting needles, size 9 (5.5 mm) **or**
size needed for gauge

GAUGE: In Stockinette Stitch,
14 sts and 23 rows = 4" (10 cm)

MUFFLER

Cast on 23 sts.

Rows 1-3: K1, (P1, K1) across.

Row 4: K1, P1, (K9, P1) twice, K1.

Row 5: K1, P1, K1, (P7, K1, P1, K1) twice.

Repeat Rows 4 and 5 for pattern until Muffler measures approximately 55¹/₂" (141 cm) from cast on edge **or to desired length minus** ¹/₂" (12 mm), ending by working Row 4.

Last 3 Rows: K1, (P1, K1) across.

Bind off all sts in pattern.

Designed by Sandy Payne.

seattle chill chasers

Jacqueline was one of Lydia's first customers. In Back on Blossom Street, *she's concerned about Alix, her good friend who's got pre-wedding jitters. She's also trying to be a good mother-in-law to Tammie Lee, who married Jacqueline's only son. This set of mock-cabled winter accessories will go to either Alix or Tammie Lee. Or maybe she will make the set twice, so they each get one!*

■■■□ INTERMEDIATE

MATERIALS

Medium Weight Yarn **④ MEDIUM**
[3.5 ounces, 195 yards
(100 grams, 175 meters) per skein]:
    Entire Set - 5 skeins
    Scarf - 3 skeins
    Hat - 1 skein
    Mittens - 1 skein
Straight knitting needles, sizes 5 (3.75 mm)
    and 7 (4.5 mm) **or** sizes needed for gauge
Yarn needle
Crochet hook (to fringe Scarf)

GAUGE: With larger size needles, in pattern,
    29 sts and 26 rows = 4" (10 cm)

Techniques used:
• YO (*Fig. 5b, page 194*)
• knit increase (*Figs. 7a & b, page 195*)
• purl increase (*Fig. 9, page 195*)
• K2 tog (*Fig. 11, page 196*)
• slip 1, K2, PSSO (*Fig. 15, page 197*)
• slip 1, K2 tog, PSSO (*Figs.16, page 197*)
• P2 tog (*Fig. 18, page 198*)

SCARF
Finished Size: 6^1/$_2$" x 67" (16.5 cm x 170 cm)

With larger size needles, cast on 47 sts.

Row 1: K2, (P3, K2) across.

Row 2 (Right side)**:** P2, (K3, P2) across.

Row 3: K2, (P3, K2) across.

Row 4: P2, ★ slip 1 as if to **knit**, K2, PSSO, P2; repeat from ★ across: 38 sts.

Row 5: K2, ★ P1, YO, P1, K2; repeat from ★ across: 47 sts.

Repeat Rows 2-5 for pattern until Scarf measures approximately 67" (170 cm) from cast on edge, ending by working Row 3.

Bind off all sts in pattern.

Holding 4 strands of yarn together, each 11" (28 cm) long, add fringe to center of each "cable" across both short ends of Scarf (*Figs. 27a & b, page 201*).

Instructions continued on page 84.

HAT

Finished Size: One size fits most adults

With larger size needles, cast on 97 sts **loosely**.

Row 1: K2, (P3, K2) across.

Row 2 (Right side): P2, (K3, P2) across.

Row 3: K2, (P3, K2) across.

Row 4: P2, ★ slip 1 as if to **knit**, K2, PSSO, P2; repeat from ★ across: 78 sts.

Row 5: K2, ★ P1, YO, P1, K2; repeat from ★ across: 97 sts.

Rows 6-53: Repeat Rows 2-5, 12 times: 97 sts.

Row 54: P2 tog, ★ slip 1 as if to **knit**, K2, PSSO, P2 tog; repeat from ★ across: 58 sts.

Row 55: K1, (P1, YO, P1, K1) across: 77 sts.

Row 56: P1, (K3, P1) across.

Row 57: K1, (P3, K1) across.

Row 58: P1, ★ slip 1 as if to **knit**, K2 tog, PSSO, P1; repeat from ★ across: 39 sts.

Row 59: K1, P2 tog across: 20 sts.

Cut yarn, leaving a long end for sewing. Thread yarn needle with end and slip remaining sts onto yarn needle, gather tightly to form a ring and secure end, then sew seam from top of Hat to last 4 "cables." Sew remaining seam in reverse so seam won't show when it's turned up.
Turn up last 4 "cables" to form cuff.

MITTEN (Make 2)
Finished Size: One size fits most adults

RIBBING
With smaller size needles, cast on 34 sts **loosely**.

Row 1: K2, (P2, K2) across.

Row 2 (Right side): P2, (K2, P2) across.

Repeat Rows 1 and 2 until Ribbing measures approximately 2$^{1}/_{2}$" (6.5 cm) from cast on edge, ending by working Row 2.

BODY
Row 1: K2, ★ P1, YO, P1, K2; repeat from ★ across: 42 sts.

Row 2 (Right side): P2, (K3, P2) across.

Row 3: K2, (P3, K2) across.

Row 4: P2, ★ slip 1 as if to **knit**, K2, PSSO, P2; repeat from ★ across: 34 sts.

Row 5: K2, (P1, YO, P1, K2) across: 42 sts.

Rows 6-43: Repeat Rows 2-5, 9 times; then repeat Rows 2 and 3 once **more**.

Row 44: P2 tog, ★ slip 1 as if to **knit**, K2, PSSO, P2 tog; repeat from ★ across: 25 sts.

Row 45: K1, (P1, YO, P1, K1) across: 33 sts.

Row 46: P1, (K3, P1) across.

Row 47: K1, (P3, K1) across.

Row 48: P1, ★ slip 1 as if to **knit**, K2 tog, PSSO, P1; repeat from ★ across: 17 sts.

Row 49: K1, P2 tog across: 9 sts.

Cut yarn, leaving a long end for sewing. Thread yarn needle with end and slip remaining sts onto yarn needle, gather tightly to form a ring and secure end, then sew seam from top of Body to last 4 "cables." Sew Ribbing from cast on edge to top of Ribbing, leaving an opening for thumb.

THUMB
With smaller size needles, cast on one st.

Row 1 (Right side): Purl increase: 2 sts.

Row 2: K1, knit increase: 3 sts.

Row 3: K1, P1, purl increase: 4 sts.

Row 4: P1, K2, purl increase: 5 sts.

Row 5: K2, P2, knit increase: 6 sts.

Row 6: P2, K2, P1, purl increase: 7 sts.

Row 7: P1, K2, P2, K1, knit increase: 8 sts.

Row 8: K1, P2, K2, P2, knit increase: 9 sts.

Row 9: (P2, K2) twice, purl increase: 10 sts.

Row 10: (K2, P2) twice, K1, knit increase: 11 sts.

Row 11: K1, (P2, K2) twice, P1, purl increase: 12 sts.

Row 12: P1, K2, (P2, K2) twice, purl increase: 13 sts.

Row 13: (K2, P2) 3 times, knit increase: 14 sts.

Row 14: (P2, K2) 3 times, P1, purl increase: 15 sts.

Row 15: P1, (K2, P2) 3 times, K1, knit increase: 16 sts.

Place a marker around the first and the last st on Row 15 to mark base of thumb seam.

Row 16: K1, P2, (K2, P2) 3 times, K1.

Row 17: P1, K2, (P2, K2) 3 times, P1.

Rows 18-23: Repeat Rows 16 and 17, 3 times.

Row 24: K1, P2, (K2 tog, P2) 3 times, K1: 13 sts.

Row 25: P1, (K2, P1) across.

Row 26: K1, (P2, K1) across.

Rows 27-30: Repeat Rows 25 and 26 twice.

Row 31: P1, K2 tog across: 7 sts.

Cut yarn, leaving a long end for sewing. Thread yarn needle with end and slip remaining sts onto yarn needle, gather tightly to form a ring and secure end, then sew seam from top of Thumb to marker at base of Thumb. Sew Thumb into opening easing to fit.

Designs by Carol Brill.

Row 6: (P1, K1) 4 times, (K2 tog, YO) 3 times, ★ (P1, K1) 3 times, (K2 tog, YO) 3 times; repeat from ★ across to last 2 sts, P1, K1.

Row 7: K1, P7, ★ K1, (P1, K1) twice, P7; repeat from ★ across to last 8 sts, (K1, P1) across.

Rows 8-15: Repeat Rows 4-7 twice.

Row 16: P1, K1, (YO, K2 tog) 3 times, ★ (P1, K1) 3 times, (YO, K2 tog) 3 times; repeat from ★ across to last 8 sts, (P1, K1) across.

Row 17: K1, (P1, K1) 3 times, P7, ★ K1, (P1, K1) twice, P7; repeat from ★ across to last 2 sts, K1, P1.

Row 18: P1, K1, (K2 tog, YO) 3 times, ★ (P1, K1) 3 times, (K2 tog, YO) 3 times; repeat from ★ across to last 8 sts, (P1, K1) across.

Row 19: K1, (P1, K1) 3 times, P7, ★ K1, (P1, K1) twice, P7; repeat from ★ across to last 2 sts, K1, P1.

Rows 20-27: Repeat Rows 16-19 twice.

Rows 28 thru 207{231-279}: Repeat Rows 4-27, 7{8-10} times; then repeat Rows 4-15 once **more**.

Bind off all sts in **knit**.

FINISHING

With **right** sides together, using diagram as a guide for placement, and matching blocks to continue checkerboard pattern, sew bound off edge of second Panel to left side of first Panel. Sew bound off edge of first Panel to edge of second Panel.

DIAGRAM

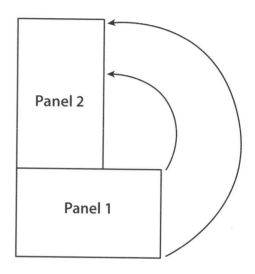

Design by Cathy Hardy.

hooded scarf

It's a fun design, and it does a great job of chasing the chill on a breezy day. Taken from Debbie's A Charity Guide for Knitters, *this hooded scarf will be welcomed by friends, family, and strangers alike. Make one for a loved one, or help someone in need keep a little warmer.*

Shown on page 91.

 EASY

Finished Measurement:
 Hood - 8" high x 18" wide (20.5 cm x 45.5 cm)
 Attached Scarf - 6" wide x 21" long
  (15 cm x 53.5 cm)

MATERIALS

 Medium Weight Yarn
 [5 ounces, 256 yards
 (142 grams, 234 meters) per skein]:
  Main Color (Blue) - 2 skeins
 [4 ounces, 204 yards
 (113 grams, 187 meters) per skein]:
  Contrasting Color (Variegated) - 1 skein
 Straight knitting needles, size 8 (5 mm)
  or size needed for gauge
 Yarn needle

GAUGE: In Stockinette Stitch,
   17 sts and 23 rows = 4" (10 cm)

Techniques used:
- adding new stitches *(Figs. 6a & b, page 195)*
- knit increase *(Figs. 7a & b, page 195)*
- K2 tog *(Fig. 11, page 196)*

RIGHT SCARF

With Main Color, cast on 25 sts **loosely**.

Rows 1-7: K1, (P1, K1) across (Seed Stitch).

Rows 8-11: With Contrasting Color, knit across (Garter Stitch stripe).

Rows 12-25: With Main Color, K1, (P1, K1) across.

Repeat Rows 8-25 for pattern until Right Scarf measures approximately 21" (53.5 cm) from cast on edge, ending by working Row 25.

Instructions continued on page 90.

HOOD

Row 1: Bind off 6 sts **loosely** in pattern, K2, knit into the front **and** into the back of each st across to last 3 sts, K3: 32 sts.

Beginning with a **purl** row, work in Stockinette Stitch (purl one row, knit one row) until Hood measures approximately 16" (40.5 cm), ending by working a **purl** row.

LEFT SCARF

Row 1: Add on 6 sts **loosely**, K1, (P1, K1) 4 times, K2 tog across to last 3 sts, K3: 25 sts.

Beginning with Row 12, work in same pattern as Right Scarf until Left Scarf measures same as Right Scarf, ending by working Row 18.

Bind off all sts **loosely** in pattern.

FRONT RIBBING

With **right** side facing, pick up 77 sts evenly spaced along Hood edge, between bound off and added on sts *(Fig. 22a, page 199)*.

Row 1: K1, (P1, K1) across.

Row 2: P1, (K1, P1) across.

Repeat Rows 1 and 2 until ribbing measures approximately 1¹/₂" (4 cm).

Bind off all sts **loosely** in ribbing.

Sew edges of Front Ribbing to Scarf.

Fold Hood in half and weave Hood seam from center to beginning of Scarf *(Fig. 23, page 199)*.

Add pom-pom to top of Hood *(Figs. 28a-c, page 201)*.

Design by Cathy Hardy.

fair isle hat & scarf

Fair Isle is a classic style of knitting that every creative person should try at least once. This hat and scarf are from Knit Along with Debbie Macomber—A Good Yarn, and they're a great place to begin. It's also best to start with a practice swatch.

MATERIALS

Fine Weight Yarn **FINE 2**

[5 ounces, 455 yards,
(140 grams, 416 meters) per skein]:

    Pink - 1 skein
    Variegated - 1 skein
    White - 1 skein
    Dk Pink - 10 yards
Straight knitting needles, sizes 3 (3.25 mm)
    and 5 (3.75 mm) **or** sizes needed
    for gauge
Crochet hook (for fringe)
Tapestry needle

GAUGE: With larger size needles,
in Stockinette Stitch,
24 sts and 32 rows = 4" (10 cm)

Technique used:
• K2 tog *(Fig. 11, page 196)*
• P2 tog *(Fig. 18, page 198)*

FAIR ISLE KNITTING

Fair Isle knitting is a Stockinette Stitch technique that uses two colors across a row. The English method of knitting (holding the yarn with the right hand) and the Continental method (holding the yarn with the left hand) can be combined for ease in changing colors. Stranding is also used, which is a method in which the color not in use is carried across the wrong side of the fabric.

To avoid carrying the yarn across 5 stitches, twist the carried color at its midpoint with the yarn in use. Make sure the carried yarn doesn't show on the right side or tighten the tension.

Drop the color you are using, lay the other color to your left on top of it, pick up the color you were using and continue working. The unused color is attached to the fabric.

Spread your stitches on the right hand needle as you knit so that you will have the correct tension on the yarn that is being carried. The stitches should be spread as much as the approximate gauge, so that the yarn carried will lie flat against the fabric. Carrying the strand slightly too loose is better than too tight, but be careful not to provide too much yarn as the stitches at end of the color section will enlarge. It's important to maintain the elasticity of the fabric. The fabric should look smooth and even on the right side without a puckered uneven appearance. The strands on the wrong side should lie flat without pulling the fabric or distorting the shape of the stitches. If the strands are pulled too tight, the gauge will also be too tight.

Instructions continued on page 94.

FOLLOWING A CHART

The chart shows each stitch as a square indicating what color each stitch should be.

Only one pattern repeat is given on the chart, and it is indicated by a blue vertical line and a bracketed indication. This section is to be repeated across the row. There is an extra stitch on each side of the repeat, indicating the first and last stitch of the row. These are edge stitches that will be woven into the seam, allowing the pattern to be continuous.

Note: On Row 9, you can knit with both Pink and Dk Pink, or add Dk Pink Duplicate Stitch later.

On **right** side rows, follow Chart from **right** to **left**; on **wrong** side rows, follow Chart from **left** to **right**.

CHART

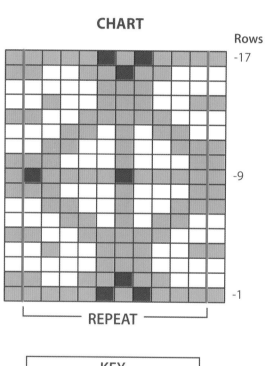

Rows
-17

-9

-1

REPEAT

KEY

- Pink
- White
- Dk Pink duplicate stitch KEY

HAT

Size	Finished Measurement
Small	16¹/₂" (42 cm)
Medium	18¹/₂" (47 cm)
Large	20" (51 cm)

Size Note: Instructions are written for size Small with sizes Medium and Large in braces { }. Instructions will be easier to read if you circle all the numbers pertaining to your size. If only one number is given, it applies to all sizes.

RIBBING

With Pink and smaller size needles, cast on 102{112-122} sts.

Work in K1, P1 ribbing for 1¹/₄" (3 cm).

BODY

Change to larger size needles.

Working in Stockinette Stitch (knit one row, purl one row) and beginning with a knit row, work 2 rows with Variegated then 2 rows with Pink.

Follow Chart.

Beginning with Pink, work even alternating 2 rows of Pink with 2 rows of Variegated until Hat measures approximately 6{6¹/₂-7}"/15{16.5-18} cm from cast on edge, ending by working a **purl** row.

CROWN

Maintain established color sequence.

Row 1: K2, ★ K2 tog, K8{9-10}; repeat from ★ across: 92{102-112} sts.

Row 2: P2, ★ P2 tog, P7{8-9}; repeat from ★ across: 82{92-102} sts.

Row 3: K2, ★ K2 tog, K6{7-8}; repeat from ★ across: 72{82-92} sts.

Continue to decrease 10 sts each row, working one less st between decreases until 20 sts remain; at end of last row, cut yarn leaving a long end for sewing.

FINISHING

Thread yarn needle with end pulling it even to make a double strand; slip remaining sts onto yarn needle; gather tightly to close Hat and secure.

Add Duplicate Stitch as indicated on Chart *(Figs. 29a & b, page 202)*.

Weave seam *(Fig. 23, page 199)*.

Weave in all yarn ends.

SCARF

Size	Finished Measurements
Small	4¼" x 40" (11 cm x 101.5 cm)
Large	5" x 50" (12.5 cm x 127 cm)

Size Note: Instructions are written for size Small with size Large in braces { }. Instructions will be easier to read if you circle all the numbers pertaining to your size. If only one number is given, it applies to all sizes.

BODY

With Pink and larger size needles, cast on 52{62} sts.

Beginning with a knit row, work 14 rows in Stockinette Stitch (knit one row, purl one row), alternating 2 rows of Pink with 2 rows of Variegated.

Follow Chart, page 94.

Beginning with Pink, work even alternating 2 rows of Pink with 2 rows of Variegated until Scarf measures approximately 36{46}"/91.5{117} cm from cast on edge, ending by working a **knit** row with Pink.

Follow Chart.

Beginning with Pink, work even for 14 rows, alternating 2 rows of Pink with 2 rows of Variegated.

Bind off all sts.

FINISHING

Add Duplicate Stitch as indicated on Chart *(Figs. 29a & b, page 202)*.

With **right** sides together, fold Body in half lengthwise and weave side seam *(Fig. 23, page 199)*; turn right side out.

Weave in all yarn ends.

Holding six 12" (30.5 cm) strands of Pink together and working through both layers, add Fringe to both ends *(Figs. 27a & b, page 201)*.

Design by Zara Zsido.

SIZES FOR WOMAN & MAN ONLY

Row 1 (Decrease row): K2, ★ P3, K2 tog; repeat from ★ across: {62-70} sts.

Row 2: ★ P1, K1, slip 1, K1; repeat from ★ across to last 2 sts, P2.

Row 3: K2, ★ P3, K1; repeat from ★ across.

Row 4 (Decrease row): ★ P1, K2 tog, K1; repeat from ★ across to last 2 sts, P2: {47-53} sts.

Row 5: K2, ★ P2, K1; repeat from ★ across.

Row 6: ★ P1, slip 1, K1; repeat from ★ across to last 2 sts, P2.

Row 7 (Decrease row): K2, ★ SSP, K1; repeat from ★ across: {32-36} sts.

Row 8: ★ P1, slip 1; repeat from ★ across to last 2 sts, P2.

Row 9: K2, ★ P1, K1; repeat from ★ across.

Row 10 (Decrease row): K2 tog across: {16-18} sts.

Row 11: Purl across.

ALL SIZES

Cut yarn leaving a long end for sewing.

Thread yarn needle with end and slip remaining sts onto yarn needle; gather tightly to close and secure end. Weave seam reversing seam on Cuff so seam won't show when it's turned up *(Fig. 23, page 199)*. Turn up bottom to form cuff.

Design by Cathy Hardy.

TOP SHAPING
SIZES FOR TODDLER & CHILD ONLY

Row 1 (Decrease row): K2, ★ P3, K2 tog; repeat from ★ across: 50{54} sts.

Row 2: ★ P1, K1, slip 1, K1; repeat from ★ across to last 2 sts, P2.

Row 3 (Decrease row): K2, ★ P1, P2 tog, K1; repeat from ★ across: 38{41} sts.

Row 4: ★ P1, slip 1, K1; repeat from ★ across to last 2 sts, P2.

Row 5 (Decrease row): K2, ★ SSP, K1; repeat from ★ across: 26{28} sts.

Row 6: ★ P1, K1; repeat from ★ across to last 2 sts, P2.

Row 7 (Decrease row): P2 tog across: 13{14} sts.

Row 8: Knit across.

a little something for you

When you need a gift that will mark a special occasion with all the affection you feel, why not knit a shawl? This pretty pattern comes from Friendship Shawls, *a collection of ten designs to knit and share.*

Shown on page 101.

■■□□ **EASY**

Finished Size: 71½" wide x 36½" deep
(181.5 cm x 92.5 cm)

MATERIALS

Medium Weight Cotton Blend Yarn [MEDIUM 4]
[3.5 ounces, 178 yards
(100 grams, 163 meters) per skein]:
   6 skeins
29" (73.5 cm) Circular knitting needle,
   size 6 (4 mm) **or** size needed for gauge

GAUGE: In pattern,
   16 sts and 24 rows = 4" (10 cm)

Gauge Swatch: 5½"w x 4¼"h (14 cm x 10.75 cm)
Cast on 22 sts.
Row 1 (Right side): Purl across.
Row 2: P1, K2, YO, slip 1 as if to **knit**, K1, PSSO,
★ P4, K2, YO, slip 1 as if to **knit**, K1, PSSO; repeat from
★ once **more**, P1.
Row 3: P3, YO, P2 tog, ★ K4, P2, YO, P2 tog; repeat
from ★ once **more**, P1.
Rows 4-25: Repeat Rows 2 and 3, 11 times.
Bind off all sts in **knit**.

Techniques used:
• YO (*Figs. 5a & b, page 194*)
• adding new sts (*Figs. 6a & b, page 195*)
• Slip 1, K1, PSSO (*Figs. 14a & b, page 197*)
• P2 tog (*Fig. 18, page 198*)

Instructions continued on page 100.

This Shawl begins at the bottom tip and is worked up. Shaping is achieved by adding on stitches in a stair-step fashion.

SHAWL

Cast on 6 sts.

Row 1 (Right side)**:** Purl across.

Row 2: P1, K2, YO, slip 1 as if to **knit**, K1, PSSO, P1.

Row 3: P3, YO, P2 tog, P1.

Rows 4-6: Repeat Rows 2 and 3 once, then repeat Row 2 once **more**.

Row 7: Add on 4 sts, P7, YO, P2 tog, P1: 10 sts.

Row 8: Add on 4 sts, P1, K2, YO, slip 1 as if to **knit**, K1, PSSO, P4, K2, YO, slip 1 as if to **knit**, K1, PSSO, P1: 14 sts.

Row 9: P3, YO, P2 tog, K4, P2, YO, P2 tog, P1.

Row 10: P1, K2, YO, slip 1 as if to **knit**, K1, PSSO, P4, K2, YO, slip 1 as if to **knit**, K1, PSSO, P1.

Rows 11 and 12: Repeat Rows 9 and 10.

Row 13: Add on 4 sts, P7, YO, P2 tog, K4, P2, YO, P2 tog, P1: 18 sts.

Row 14: Add on 4 sts, P1, K2, YO, slip 1 as if to **knit**, K1, PSSO, ★ P4, K2, YO, slip 1 as if to **knit**, K1, PSSO; repeat from ★ across to last st, P1: 22 sts.

Row 15: P3, YO, P2 tog, ★ K4, P2, YO, P2 tog; repeat from ★ across to last st, P1.

Row 16: P1, K2, YO, slip 1 as if to **knit**, K1, PSSO, ★ P4, K2, YO, slip 1 as if to **knit**, K1, PSSO; repeat from ★ across to last st, P1.

Rows 17 and 18: Repeat Rows 15 and 16.

Row 19: Add on 4 sts, P7, YO, P2 tog, ★ K4, P2, YO, P2 tog; repeat from ★ across to last st, P1: 26 sts.

Repeat Rows 14-19 for pattern until Shawl measures approximately 71^1/$_2$" (181.5 cm) across top edge **or** to desired size, ending by working Row 18; then repeat Row 15 once **more**.

Last 4 Rows: Purl across.

Bind off all sts in **purl**.

Design by Cathy Hardy.

cowl

Dress it up or dress it down, this pretty cowl is fun to knit and easy to wear. Inspired by Debbie's book, A Turn in the Road, *the pattern is mostly Stockinette Stitch on circular needles, making it a perfect take-along project whenever you travel.*

 **BEGINNER +**

Finished Size: 13" high x 26" circumference
(33 cm x 66 cm)

MATERIALS

Light Weight Yarn **LIGHT 3**
[3.5 ounces, 253 yards
(100 grams, 230 meters) per skein]:
1 skein
24" (61 cm) Circular knitting needle, size
6 (4 mm) **or** size needed for gauge
Marker

GAUGE: In Stockinette Stitch,
21 sts and 27 rnds/rows = 4" (10 cm)

BOTTOM BORDER

Cast on 136 sts *(Fig. 1a, page 192)*; place marker to indicate the beginning of the round *(see Markers, page 191)*.

Rnds 1-4: ★ K4, P4; repeat from ★ around.

Rnds 5-8: ★ P4, K4; repeat from ★ around.

BODY

Remove marker and knit around for Stockinette Stitch until piece measures approximately 12" (30.5 cm) from cast on edge **or** 1" (2.5 cm) less than desired height.

TOP BORDER

Rnds 1-8: Place marker and work same as Bottom Border.

Bind off all sts in pattern.

Design by Cathy Hardy.

a wisp of warmth

So delicate and airy, this wrap will make the wearer feel truly special. It's the perfect accessory for when just the lightest touch of warmth is needed, and it's one of the thoughtful designs in Debbie's pattern book, Friendship Shawls.

Finished Size: Unblocked 55" (139.5 cm) diameter, blocked 70" (178 cm)

MATERIALS

Super Fine Wool Yarn 【SUPER FINE 1】
[1.75 ounces, 440 yards
(50 grams, 402 meters) per hank]:
   4 hanks
Set of four, 8" (20.5 cm) double pointed
   knitting needles, size 6 (4 mm) **or** size
   needed for gauge
16" (40.5 cm), 24" (61 cm) and 36" (91.5 cm)
   Circular knitting needles, size 6 (4 mm) **or**
   size needed for gauge
Split ring marker
Markers
Pins for blocking
optional flexible blocking wires

Yarn Note: Wool was chosen to make this lacy shawl. It will help it stretch during the blocking process.

GAUGE: In Stockinette Stitch, 24 sts = 4" (10 cm)

Techniques used:
• YO (*Fig. 5a, page 194*)
• M1 (*Figs. 10a & b, page 196*)
• K2 tog (*Fig. 11, page 196*)
• K2 tog tbl (*Fig. 12, page 196*)
• SSK (*Figs. 13a-c, page 196*)

This Shawl is worked in rounds, forming a large circle. You will begin using double pointed needles and change to a circular needle when the stitches become crowded.

The charts, page 107, can be used along with the instructions (*see Following Lace Charts, page 191*).

SHAWL

Cast 9 sts loosely onto a double pointed needle; transfer 3 sts onto each of 2 other double pointed needles (*see Double Pointed Needles, page 193*): 3 sts each needle (9 sts total).

Note: Place a split ring marker at the beginning of the first cast on stitch to mark the beginning of the round. Begin working in rounds, making sure that the first round is not twisted.

Instructions continued on page 106.

Rnd 1: Knit across each needle.

Note: If there is a YO at the end of each needle, take care not to drop it.

Rnd 2: (K1, YO) across each needle: 6 sts on each needle (18 sts total).

Rnds 3-5: Knit across each needle.

Rnd 6: (K1, YO) across each needle: 12 sts on each needle (36 sts total).

Rnds 7-9: Knit across each needle.

Rnd 10: (K2 tog, YO) across each needle.

Rnds 11-13: Knit across each needle.

Rnd 14: (K1, YO) across each needle: 24 sts on each needle (72 sts total).

Rnds 15 and 16: Knit across each needle.

Rnd 17: (K 12, M1, K 12) across each needle: 25 sts on each needle (75 sts total).

Rnd 18: Knit across each needle.

Rnd 19: ★ K2 tog, YO, K1, YO, SSK; repeat from ★ across each needle.

Rnd 20: Knit across each needle.

Rnds 21-23: Repeat Rnds 19 and 20 once, then repeat Rnd 19 once **more**.

Rnds 24-27: Knit across each needle.

Note: At this point you may be able to replace the double pointed needles with a 16" (40.5 cm) circular needle. When working the next round, place markers as indicated *(see Markers, page 191)*, making sure that the beginning marker is a different color or type to mark the beginning of the rounds. Instructions will now reflect that change by working around.

Rnd 28: (K1, YO) around placing a marker after every 30 sts: 30 sts in each of 5 sections (150 sts total).

Rnds 29-32: Knit around.

Rnd 33: ★ K2 tog, YO, K1, YO, SSK; repeat from ★ around.

Rnd 34: Knit around.

Rnds 35-37: Repeat Rnds 33 and 34 once, then repeat Rnd 33 once **more**.

Rnds 38-41: Knit around.

Rnd 42: (K2 tog, YO) around.

Rnds 43-55: Repeat Rnds 29-41.

Rnd 56: (K1, YO) around: 60 sts in each section (300 sts total).

Rnds 57-111: Repeat Rnds 29-42, 3 times; then repeat Rnds 29-41 once **more**.

Rnd 112: (K1, YO) around placing additional markers to have a marker every 60 sts: 60 sts in each of 10 sections (600 sts total).

Rnds 113-204: Repeat Rnds 29-42, 6 times; then repeat Rnds 29-36 once **more**.

Rnd 205: ★ K2 tog, YO, K1, YO, SSK, YO; repeat from ★ around: 72 sts in each section (720 sts total).

Bind off all sts as follows: K2, return the 2 sts just knit back onto left needle, knit these 2 sts together through back loop, ★ K1, return the 2 sts on right needle back onto left needle, knit these 2 sts together through back loop; repeat from ★ around; finish off.

Wash and block Shawl *(see Blocking, page 200)*. You can use flexible blocking wires that are stainless steel and rustproof to block your Shawl. Simply insert the wire along the edge of your Shawl and pin the Shawl as needed to your blocking board.

Design by Kay Meadors.

CHART

Repeat

KEY

◯ YO

╱ K2 tog

╲ SSK

☐ Knit

▨ No stitch in this area

When working with Purple or Brown, carry Rose loosely on the **wrong** side.

Row 5 (Right side): P1, K1, P3, with Brown K2, with Rose K1, with Purple K2, with Rose P3, (K1, P1) twice.

Maintain colors on established stitches throughout Cable Panel.

When changing colors, always pick up the new color yarn from **beneath** the dropped yarn and keep the color which has just been worked to the left of it *(Fig. 3b, page 193)*. This will prevent holes in the finished piece. Take extra care to keep your tension even.

Row 6: P1, K1, P2, K3, P5, K3, P1, K1.

To work Cable (uses 5 sts)**:** Slip next 3 sts onto cable needle and hold in **front** of work, K2 from left needle, slip Rose st from cable needle back onto left needle and knit it, K2 from cable needle.

Row 7: P1, K1, P3, work Cable, P3, (K1, P1) twice.

Row 8: P1, K1, P2, K3, P5, K3, P1, K1.

Row 9: P1, K1, P3, K5, P3, (K1, P1) twice.

Row 10: P1, K1, P2, K3, P5, K3, P1, K1.

Row 11: P1, K1, P3, K2, (K, P, K, P, K) **all** in next st, pass second, third, fourth, and fifth sts on right needle over first st, K2, P3, (K1, P1) twice.

Row 12: P1, K1, P2, K3, P5, K3, P1, K1.

Row 13: P1, K1, P3, K5, P3, (K1, P1) twice.

Row 14: P1, K1, P2, K3, P5, K3, P1, K1.

Repeat Rows 7-14 for pattern until Panel measures approximately 71^1/$_2$" (181.5 cm) from cast on edge, ending by working Row 8.

Cut Purple and Brown.

Next Row: With Rose, K5, slip 1 as if to **knit**, K1, PSSO, K1, K2 tog, K7: 15 sts.

Last 3 Rows: Knit across.

Bind off all sts in **knit**.

PATTERN 1

Note: To pick up and knit stitches, pick up a stitch *(Fig. 22a, page 199)* and place it on the left needle, then knit the stitch.

With **right** side facing, using circular needle and Purple, and beginning at cast on edge, pick up and knit 324 sts evenly spaced across right edge of Cable Panel.

Row 1: Knit across; do **not** cut Purple.

Carry unused yarn along side edge.

Row 2: With Rose, knit across.

Row 3: K3, ★ P3 tog leaving sts on needle, YO, purl same 3 sts together again slipping sts off left needle; repeat from ★ across to last 3 sts, K3.

Rows 4 and 5: With Purple, knit across.

Repeat Rows 2-5 for pattern until Pattern 1 measures approximately 8" (20.5 cm), ending by working Row 5.

Cut Purple; do **not** cut Rose.

Instructions continued on page 112.

PATTERN 2

Row 1: With Rose, K8, M1, (K7, M1) across to last 8 sts, K8: 369 sts.

Row 2: K3, (P3, K3) across.

To work Right Twist (uses 3 sts)**:** Working in **front** of the piece, knit the third st on the left needle without slipping it off *(Fig. A)*, then knit the first 2 sts on the left needle slipping all 3 sts off the left needle.

Fig. A

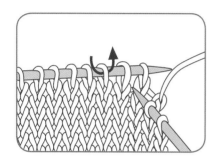

Row 3: With Rose, K3, (work Right Twist, K3) across.

Row 4: K3, (P3, K3) across.

When instructed to slip stitches, always slip as if to **purl** with yarn held on the **wrong** side.

Rows 5 and 6: With Brown, K3, (slip 3, K3) across.

Repeat Rows 3-6 for pattern until Pattern 2 measures approximately 6" (15 cm), ending by working Row 6.

Cut Brown.

Last 4 Rows: Repeat Rows 3 and 4 twice.

Do **not** cut Rose.

PATTERN 3

Row 1: With Purple, (K6, K2 tog) 4 times, K5, ★ K2 tog, K6, K2 tog, K5; repeat from ★ across to last 32 sts, (K2 tog, K6) 4 times: 321 sts.

Row 2: Knit across.

Row 3: With Brown, knit across.

Row 4: K3, ★ P3 tog leaving sts on needle, YO, purl same 3 sts together again slipping sts off left needle; repeat from ★ across to last 3 sts, K3.

Rows 5 and 6: With Purple, knit across.

Row 7: With Rose, knit across.

Row 8: Purl across.

Rows 9 and 10: With Purple, knit across.

Rows 11-15: Repeat Rows 3-7.

Cut Brown and Purple.

PATTERN 4

Rows 1-6: K3, P1, (K1, P1) across to last 3 sts, K3.

Bind off all sts in pattern.

Design by Cathy Hardy.

reese's vest

In Summer on Blossom Street, *Jacqueline Donovan returns from a cruise with her husband Reese and goes straight to Lydia's yarn shop. Jacqueline is looking for the perfect yarn to make a vest for Reese. Any knitter who makes this design will love watching the intricate pattern form.*

Shown on page 115.

Shown on page 115.

▪▪▪▫ INTERMEDIATE

	Finished Chest	
Size	**Measurement**	
34	36"	(91.5 cm)
36	38"	(96.5 cm)
38	40"	(101.5 cm)
40	42½"	(108 cm)
42	44"	(112 cm)
44	46"	(117 cm)

Size Note: Instructions are written with sizes 34, 36, and 38 in the first set of braces { } and sizes 40, 42, and 44 in the second set of braces. Instructions will be easier to read if you circle all the numbers pertaining to your size. If only one number is given, it applies to all sizes.

GAUGE: With larger size needle, in Reverse Stockinette Stitch, 23 sts and 30 rows = 4" (10 cm)

Techniques used:
• tbl *(Fig. 4, page 193)*
• knit increase *(Figs. 7a & b, page 195)*
• K2 tog *(Fig. 11, page 196)*
• SSK *(Figs. 13a-c, page 196)*
• P2 tog *(Fig. 18, page 198)*
• SSP *(Fig. 21, page 198)*

Instructions continued on page 114.

MATERIALS

Fine Weight Yarn 🧶**FINE 2**
[1.75 ounces, 110 yards
(50 grams, 101 meters) per skein]:
{6-7-7}{7-8-8} skeins
Straight knitting needles, sizes 2 (2.75 mm)
  and 3 (3.25 mm) **or** sizes needed for gauge
16" (40.5 cm) Circular knitting needle,
  size 2 (2.75 mm)
Cable needle
Markers
Tapestry needle

STITCH GUIDE

TWIST 2 LEFT
Slip next st onto cable needle and hold in **front** of work, P1 from left needle, K1 tbl from cable needle.

TWIST 2 RIGHT
Slip next st onto cable needle and hold in **back** of work, K1 tbl from left needle, P1 from cable needle.

TWIST 2
Slip next st onto cable needle and hold in **back** of work, P1 tbl from left needle, P1 tbl from cable neede.

FRONT
RIBBING
With smaller size needles, cast on {106-112-118}{124-128-134} sts.

Work in K1, P1 ribbing for 14 rows.

Next Row (Increase row): Work across {39-42-45}{48-50-53} sts in established ribbing, place marker **(see Markers, page 191)**, knit into the front **and** into the back of the next st, (work across 8 sts, knit into the front **and** into the back of the next st) 3 times, place marker, work across last {39-42-45}{48-50-53} sts: {110-116-122}{128-132-138} sts.

BODY
Change to larger size needles.

Row 1 (Right side): Purl across to marker, ★ twist 2 left twice, P2, twist 2 right, twist 2 left, P2, twist 2 right twice; repeat from ★ once **more**, purl across.

Row 2: Knit across to marker, (K1, P1 tbl) twice, (K2, P1 tbl) 3 times, (K1, P1 tbl, K2, P1 tbl) twice, (K2, P1 tbl) twice, K1, P1 tbl, knit across.

Row 3: Purl across to marker, P1, † twist 2 left twice, twist 2 right, P2, twist 2 left, twist 2 right twice †, P2, repeat from † to † once, purl across.

Row 4: Knit across to marker, K2, † P1 tbl, K1, P2 tbl, K4, P2 tbl, K1, P1 tbl †, K4, repeat from † to † once, knit across.

Row 5: Purl across to marker, P2, twist 2 left twice, P4, twist 2 right twice, P4, twist 2 left twice, P4, twist 2 right twice, purl across.

Row 6: Knit across to marker, K3, P1 tbl, K1, P1 tbl, K4, P1 tbl, K1, P2 tbl, K4, P2 tbl, K1, P1 tbl, K4, P1 tbl, K1, P1 tbl, knit across.

Row 7: Purl across to marker, P3, twist 2 left twice, P2, twist 2 right twice, twist 2 left, P2, twist 2 right, twist 2 left twice, P2, twist 2 right twice, purl across.

Row 8: Knit across to marker, K4, (P1 tbl, K1, P1 tbl, K2) twice, P1 tbl, K2, P1 tbl, (K2, P1 tbl, K1, P1 tbl) twice, knit across.

Row 9: Purl across to marker, P4, twist 2 left twice, twist 2 right twice, P2, twist 2 left, twist 2 right, P2, twist 2 left twice, twist 2 right twice, purl across.

Row 10: Knit across to marker, K5, † P1 tbl, K1, twist 2, K1, P1 tbl †, K4, twist 2, K4, repeat from † to † once, knit across.

Row 11: Purl across to marker, P4, twist 2 right twice, twist 2 left twice, P2, twist 2 right, twist 2 left, P2, twist 2 right twice, twist 2 left twice, purl across.

Row 12: Knit across to marker, K4, (P1 tbl, K1, P1 tbl, K2) twice, P1 tbl, K2, P1 tbl, (K2, P1 tbl, K1, P1 tbl) twice, knit across.

Instructions continued on page 116.

Row 13: Purl across to marker, P3, twist 2 right twice, P2, twist 2 left twice, twist 2 right, P2, twist 2 left, twist 2 right twice, P2, twist 2 left twice, purl across.

Row 14: Knit across to marker, K3, P1 tbl, K1, P1 tbl, K4, P1 tbl, K1, P2 tbl, K4, P2 tbl, K1, P1 tbl, K4, P1 tbl, K1, P1 tbl, knit across.

Row 15: Purl across to marker, P2, twist 2 right twice, P4, twist 2 left twice, P4, twist 2 right twice, P4, twist 2 left twice, purl across.

Row 16: Knit across to marker, K2, † P1 tbl, K1, P2 tbl, K4, P2 tbl, K1, P1 tbl †, K4, repeat from † to † once, knit across.

Row 17: Purl across to marker, P1, † twist 2 right twice, twist 2 left, P2, twist 2 right, twist 2 left twice †, P2, repeat from † to † once, purl across.

Row 18: Knit across to marker, (K1, P1 tbl) twice, (K2, P1 tbl) 3 times, (K1, P1 tbl, K2, P1 tbl) twice, (K2, P1 tbl) twice, K1, P1 tbl, knit across.

Row 19: Purl across to marker, ★ twist 2 right twice, P2, twist 2 left, twist 2 right, P2, twist 2 left twice; repeat from ★ once **more**, purl across.

Row 20: Knit across to marker, P1 tbl, K1, P1 tbl, K4, twist 2, K4, P1 tbl, K1, twist 2, K1, P1 tbl, K4, twist 2, K4, P1 tbl, K1, P1 tbl, knit across.

Rows 21 thru {92-90-90}{88-88-86}: Repeat Rows 1-20, 3 times; then repeat Rows 1 thru {12-10-10}{8-8-6} once **more**.

ARMHOLE SHAPING
Maintain established pattern throughout.

Rows 1 and 2: Bind off {7-7-8}{8-9-10} sts, work across: {96-102-106}{112-114-118} sts.

Row 3 (Decrease row): P1, P2 tog, work across to last 3 sts, SSP, P1: {94-100-104}{110-112-116} sts.

Row 4 (Decrease row): K1, SSK, work across to last 3 sts, K2 tog, K1: {92-98-102}{108-110-114} sts.

Continue to decrease one stitch at **each** Armhole edge, every row {1-1-2}{2-2-3} time(s) **more**; then decrease every other row, {4-4-4}{5-5-5} times: {82-88-90}{94-96-98} sts.

Work even until a total of six, 20-row repeats (120 rows) have been completed above the ribbing and ending by working pattern Row 20.

NECK SHAPING
Both sides of Neck are worked at the same time using separate yarn for **each** side.

Row 1: Purl across to within 2 sts of marker, SSP, † twist 2 left twice, P2, twist 2 right, twist 2 left, P2, twist 2 right twice †; with second yarn, repeat from † to † once, P2 tog, purl across: {40-43-44}{46-47-48} sts **each** side.

Row 2: Knit across to marker, † (K1, P1 tbl) twice, (K2, P1 tbl) 3 times, K1, P1 tbl, K1 †; with second yarn, repeat from † to † once, knit across.

Row 3: Purl across to within 2 sts of marker, SSP, † P1, twist 2 left twice, twist 2 right, P2, twist 2 left, twist 2 right twice, P1 †; with second yarn, repeat from † to † once, P2 tog, purl across: {39-42-43}{45-46-47} sts **each** side.

Row 4: Knit across to marker, † K2, P1 tbl, K1, P2 tbl, K4, P2 tbl, K1, P1 tbl, K2 †; with second yarn, repeat from † to † once, knit across.

Row 5: Purl across to within 2 sts of marker, SSP, † P2, twist 2 left twice, P4, twist 2 right twice, P2 †; with second yarn, repeat from † to † once, P2 tog, purl across: {38-41-42}{44-45-46} sts **each** side.

Row 6: Knit across to marker, † K3, P1 tbl, K1, P1 tbl, K4, P1 tbl, K1, P1 tbl, K3 †; with second yarn, repeat from † to † once, knit across.

Row 7: Purl across to within 2 sts of marker, SSP, † P3, twist 2 left twice, P2, twist 2 right twice, P3 †; with second yarn, repeat from † to † once, P2 tog, purl across: {37-40-41}{43-44-45} sts **each** side.

Row 8: Knit across to marker, † K4, P1 tbl, K1, P1 tbl, K2, P1 tbl, K1, P1 tbl, K4 †; with second yarn, repeat from † to † once, knit across.

Row 9: Purl across to within 2 sts of marker, SSP, † P4, twist 2 left twice, twist 2 right twice, P4 †; with second yarn, repeat from † to † once, P2 tog, purl across: {36-39-40}{42-43-44} sts **each** side.

Row 10: Knit across to marker, † K5, P1 tbl, K1, twist 2, K1, P1 tbl, K5 †; with second yarn, repeat from † to † once, knit across.

Row 11: Purl across to within 2 sts of marker, SSP, † P4, twist 2 right twice, twist 2 left twice, P4 †; with second yarn, repeat from † to † once, P2 tog, purl across: {35-38-39}{41-42-43} sts **each** side.

Row 12: Knit across to marker, † K4, P1 tbl, K1, P1 tbl, K2, P1 tbl, K1, P1 tbl, K4 †; with second yarn, repeat from † to † once, knit across.

Row 13: Purl across to within 2 sts of marker, SSP, † P3, twist 2 right twice, P2, twist 2 left twice, P3 †; with second yarn, repeat from † to † once, P2 tog, purl across: {34-37-38}{40-41-42} sts **each** side.

Row 14: Knit across to marker, † K3, P1 tbl, K1, P1 tbl, K4, P1 tbl, K1, P1 tbl, K3 †; with second yarn, repeat from † to † once, knit across.

Row 15: Purl across to within 2 sts of marker, SSP, † P2, twist 2 right twice, P4, twist 2 left twice, P2 †; with second yarn, repeat from † to † once, P2 tog, purl across: {33-36-37}{39-40-41} sts **each** side.

Row 16: Knit across to marker, † K2, P1 tbl, K1, P2 tbl, K4, P2 tbl, K1, P1 tbl, K2 †; with second yarn, repeat from † to † once, knit across.

Instructions continued on page 118.

Row 17: Purl across to within 2 sts of marker, SSP, † P1, twist 2 right twice, twist 2 left, P2, twist 2 right, twist 2 left twice, P1 †; with second yarn, repeat from † to † once, P2 tog, purl across: {32-35-36}{38-39-40} sts **each** side.

Row 18: Knit across to marker, † (K1, P1 tbl) twice, (K2, P1 tbl) 3 times, K1, P1 tbl, K1 †; with second yarn, repeat from † to † once, knit across.

Row 19: Purl across to within 2 sts of marker, SSP, † twist 2 right twice, P2, twist 2 left, twist 2 right, P2, twist 2 left twice †; with second yarn, repeat from † to † once, P2 tog, purl across: {31-34-35}{37-38-39} sts **each** side.

Row 20: Knit across to marker, † P1 tbl, K1, P1 tbl, K4, twist 2, K4, P1 tbl, K1, P1 tbl †; with second yarn, repeat from † to † once, knit across.

Continue to repeat Rows 1-20 for pattern, decreasing one stitch at **each** neck edge in same manner, every other row, {2-4-5}{5-6-6} times **more**, then decrease every fourth row, {5-4-4}{4-4-4} times: {24-26-26}{28-28-29} sts **each** side.

Next 2 Rows: Work even.

Last Row: Work across decreasing 2 sts evenly spaced across the 16 pattern sts on **each** side: {22-24-24}{26-26-27} sts **each** side.

Bind off all sts in **purl**.

BACK
RIBBING
With smaller size needles, cast on {106-112-118}{124-128-134} sts.

Work in K1, P1 ribbing for 15 rows.

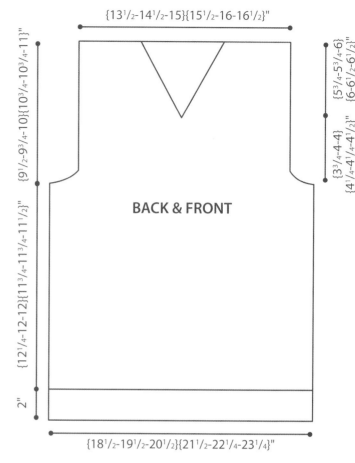

Note: Vest includes two edge stitches.

BODY
Change to larger size needles.

Beginning with a **purl** row, work in Reverse Stockinette Stitch until Back measures same as Front to Armhole Shaping, ending by working a **knit** row.

ARMHOLE SHAPING
Rows 1 and 2: Bind off {7-7-8}{8-9-10} sts, work across: {92-98-102}{108-110-114} sts.

Row 3 (Decrease row): P1, P2 tog, purl across to last 3 sts, SSP, P1: {90-96-100}{106-108-112} sts.

Row 4 (Decrease row): K1, SSK, knit across to last 3 sts, K2 tog, K1: {88-94-98}{104-106-110} sts.

Continue to decrease one stitch at **each** Armhole edge, every row {1-1-2}{2-2-3} time(s) **more**; then decrease every other row, {4-4-4}{5-5-5} times: {78-84-86}{90-92-94} sts.

Work even until Back measures same as Front, ending by working a **knit** row.

Bind off all sts in **purl**.

FINISHING
Sew shoulder seams.

NECK RIBBING
With **right** side facing and using circular needle, pick up {34-34-36}{36-38-38} sts evenly spaced along left Front Neck edge *(Fig. 22a, page 199)*, place marker, pick up {33-33-35}{35-37-37} sts evenly spaced along right Front Neck edge, pick up {34-36-38}{38-40-40} sts evenly spaced across Back, place marker to mark beginning of rnd: {101-103-109}{109-115-115} sts.

Rnd 1 (Decrease rnd): (K1, P1) across to within 2 sts of next marker, K2 tog, SSK, P1, (K1, P1) around: {99-101-107}{107-113-113} sts.

Rnds 2 and 3 (Decrease rnds): Work in established ribbing across to within 2 sts of next marker, K2 tog, SSK, work in established ribbing around: {95-97-103}{103-109-109} sts.

Bind off all sts in ribbing.

ARMHOLE RIBBING
With **right** side facing and using smaller size straight needles, pick up {108-114-114}{120-124-126} sts evenly spaced along Armhole edge.

Work in K1, P1 ribbing for 3 rows.

Bind off all sts in ribbing.

Repeat for second Armhole.

Weave side seams *(Fig. 23, page 199)*.

Design by Cathy Hardy.

cable slippers

When Bethanne returns from her travels in A Turn in the Road, *she may very well put on a pair of knitted slippers like these so she can just relax. This warm pattern is knitted while holding two yarn strands together.*

■■■□□ **EASY +**

Size	Finished Foot Circumference		Finished Length	
Small	8"	(20.5 cm)	9"	(23 cm)
Medium	8³/₄"	(22 cm)	10"	(25.5 cm)
Large	9¹/₄"	(23.5 cm)	11"	(28 cm)

Size Note: Instructions are written for size Small with sizes Medium and Large in braces { }. Instructions will be easier to read if you circle all the numbers pertaining to your size. If only one number is given, it applies to all sizes.

MATERIALS
Medium Weight Yarn **MEDIUM 4**
[4 ounces, 203 yards
(113 grams, 186 meters) per skein]:
  2 skeins
Straight knitting needles, sizes 8 (5 mm) **and**
  10 (6 mm) **or** sizes needed for gauge
Cable needle
Stitch holder
Yarn needle

Slippers are made holding 2 strands of yarn together throughout.

GAUGE: With larger size needles,
        in Seed Stitch,
        12 sts and 20 rows = 4" (10 cm)

Gauge Swatch: 4" (10 cm) square
With larger size needles, cast on 12 sts.
Row 1: (K1, P1) across.
Row 2: (P1, K1) across.
Rows 3-20: Repeat Rows 1 and 2, 9 times.
Bind off all sts.

Techniques used:
• knit increase *(Figs. 7a & b, page 195)*
• M1 *(Figs. 10a & b, page 196)*
• K2 tog *(Fig. 11, page 196)*
• Slip 1, K1, PSSO *(Figs. 14a & b, page 197)*
• P2 tog *(Fig. 18, page 198)*

STICH GUIDE

BACK CABLE (uses 4 sts)
Slip next 2 sts onto cable needle and hold in **back** of work, K2 from left needle, K2 from cable needle.
FRONT CABLE (uses 4 sts)
Slip next 2 sts onto cable needle and hold in **front** of work, K2 from left needle, K2 from cable needle.
BACK TWIST (uses 4 sts)
Slip next 2 sts onto cable needle and hold in **back** of work, K2 from left needle, P2 from cable needle.
FRONT TWIST (uses 4 sts)
Slip next 2 sts onto cable needle and hold in **front** of work, P2 from left needle, K2 from cable needle.

Instructions continued on page 122.

TOP

FIRST SIDE

With larger size needles, cast on 11 sts.

Row 1: P1, K2, P4, K3, P1.

Row 2 (Right side)**:** K1, P3, K4, P2, K1.

Row 3: P1, K2, P4, K3, P1.

Row 4: K1, P3, work Back Cable, P2, K1.

Repeat Rows 1-4 for pattern until First Side measures approximately 4$\frac{1}{2}${5$\frac{1}{2}$-6$\frac{1}{2}$}"/11.5{14-16.5} cm from cast on edge, ending by working Row 4.

Slip sts onto st holder; cut yarn.

SECOND SIDE

With larger size needles, cast on 11 sts.

Row 1: P1, K3, P4, K2, P1.

Row 2 (Right side)**:** K1, P2, K4, P3, K1.

Row 3: P1, K3, P4, K2, P1.

Row 4: K1, P2, work Front Cable, P3, K1.

Repeat Rows 1-4 for pattern until Second Side measures same as First Side, ending by working Row 4.

INSTEP

Row 1 (Joining row)**:** P1, K3, P4, K1, K2 tog; slip sts from st holder (First Side) onto empty needle, with **wrong** side facing, slip 1 as if to **knit**, K1, PSSO, K1, P4, K3, P1: 20 sts.

Row 2: K1, P3, K4, P4, K4, P3, K1.

Row 3: P1, K3, P4, K4, P4, K3, P1.

Row 4: K1, M1, P3, work Back Cable, P4, work Front Cable, P3, M1, K1: 22 sts.

Row 5: P1, K4, (P4, K4) twice, P1.

Row 6: K1, P2, (work Back Twist, work Front Twist) twice, P2, K1.

Row 7: P1, K2, P2, K4, P4, K4, P2, K2, P1.

Row 8: K1, P2, K2, P4, work Front Cable, P4, K2, P2, K1.

Row 9: P1, K2, P2, K4, P4, K4, P2, K2, P1.

Row 10: K1, P2, K2, P4, K4, P4, K2, P2, K1.

Rows 11-13: Repeat Rows 7-9.

Row 14: K1, P2, (work Front Twist, work Back Twist) twice, P2, K1.

Row 15: P1, K4, (P4, K4) twice, P1.

Row 16: K1, P2 tog, P2, work Front Cable, P4, work Back Cable, P2, P2 tog, K1: 20 sts.

Row 17: P1, K3, P4, K4, P4, K3, P1.

Row 18: K1, P2 tog, P1, K2, work Front Twist, work Back Twist, K2, P1, P2 tog, K1: 18 sts.

Row 19: P1, K2, P2, K2, P4, K2, P2, K2, P1.

Row 20: K1, P2, K2, P2, work Front Cable, P2, K2, P2, K1.

Row 21: P1, K2, P2, K2, P4, K2, P2, K2, P1.

Row 22: K1, P2, K2, P2, K4, P2, K2, P2, K1.

Row 23: P1, K2, P2, K2, P4, K2, P2, K2, P1.

Row 24: K1, P2 tog, K2 tog, P2 tog, work Front Cable, P2 tog, K2 tog, P2 tog, K1: 12 sts.

Row 25: P2 tog across; cut yarn leaving a long end for sewing: 6 sts.

Thread yarn needle with end and slip remaining sts onto yarn needle; gather tightly and secure end.

SOLE

With larger size needles and leaving a long end for sewing, cast on 7{8-9} sts.

Row 1: Purl across.

Row 2 (Right side): Knit increase in each st across: 14{16-18} sts.

Note: Loop a short piece of yarn around any stitch to mark Row 2 as **right** side and heel.

Row 3: P2, (K1, P1) across.

Row 4: K2, (P1, K1) across.

Repeat Rows 3 and 4 for Seed Stitch until Sole measures approximately 9{10-11}"/23{25.5-28} cm from cast on edge, ending by working Row 4.

Last Row: P2 tog across; cut yarn leaving a long end for sewing: 7{8-9} sts.

Thread yarn needle with end and slip remaining sts onto yarn needle; gather tightly and secure end.

Thread yarn needle with end at cast on edge. To form the heel, weave needle through cast on sts; gather tightly, allowing heel to cup, and secure yarn.

FINISHING
RIBBING

With smaller size needles and **right** sides facing, pick up 40{44-48} sts evenly spaced along end of rows at inside edge of Sides *(Fig. 22a, page 199)*.

Work in K1, P1 ribbing for 2" (5 cm).

Bind off all sts loosely leaving a long end for sewing.

Using a single strand of yarn, weave Ribbing and cast on edges of Sides together *(Fig. 23, page 199)*; sew Top to Sole.

Design by Cathy Hardy.

socks

Unless you live in the tropics where it never gets cold, someone near you could really use a pair of warm socks like these. They are one of eighteen designs in Debbie's pattern book, A Charity Guide for Knitters. The pattern is written in three sizes for adults.

■■■□ INTERMEDIATE

Adult Size	Finished Foot Circumference	
Small	8"	(20.5 cm)
Medium	9"	(23 cm)
Large	10¼"	(26 cm)

Size Note: Instructions are written for size Small with sizes Medium and Large in braces { }. Instructions will be easier to read if you circle all the numbers pertaining to your size. If only one number is given, it applies to all sizes.

MATERIALS

Super Fine Weight Self Striping Yarn
[3.5 ounces, 425 yards
(100 grams, 388 meters) per skein]: 1 skein
Set of 5 double pointed knitting needles,
    sizes 3 (3.25 mm) **and** 4 (3.5 mm) **or** sizes
    needed for gauge
Stitch holders - 2
Split-ring marker
Tapestry needle

Yarn Note: Since a tight gauge is desirable for warmth, a fine weight yarn can be substituted as long as gauge is obtained.

GAUGE: With smaller size needles,
    in Stockinette Stitch,
    28 sts and 36 rnds = 4" (10 cm)

Techniques used:
• K2 tog *(Fig. 11, page 196)*
• SSK *(Figs. 13a-c, page 196)*
• P2 tog *(Fig. 18, page 198)*

LEG
With larger size needle, cast on 56{64-72} sts.

Slip 14{16-18} sts onto each of 4 double pointed needles *(see Double Pointed Needles, page 193)*.

Note: The yarn end indicates the beginning of the round.

Rnd 1: ★ K3, P1, (K1, P1) twice; repeat from ★ around.

Rnd 2: ★ K3, P2, K1, P2; repeat from ★ around.

Repeat Rnds 1 and 2 until Leg measures approximately 2{2½-3}"/5{6.5-7.5} cm from cast on edge.

Change to smaller size needles.

Continue to repeat Rnds 1 and 2 for pattern until Leg measures approximately 6{7-8}"/15{18-20.5} cm from cast on edge **or** 1" (2.5 cm) less than desired length.

Knit each round (Stockinette Stitch) for 1" (2.5 cm).

Instructions continued on page 126.

HEEL FLAP

Dividing Stitches: Knit across first needle; slip sts from the next 2 needles onto 2 separate st holders for Instep to be worked later; **turn.**

Note: The following pattern will make the Heel dense and will help prevent it from wearing out.

With **wrong** side facing, work Row 1 across both needles onto one needle. The Heel Flap will be worked back and forth across these 28{32-36} sts.

When instructed to slip a stitch, always slip as if to **purl** with yarn held to **wrong** side.

Row 1: ★ Slip 1, P1; repeat from ★ across.

Row 2: ★ Slip 1, K1; repeat from ★ across.

Repeat Rows 1 and 2, 13{15-17} times; then repeat Row 1 once **more.**

TURN HEEL

Begin working in short rows as follows:

Row 1: Slip 1, K 16{20-24}, SSK, K1, leave remaining 8 sts unworked; **turn.**

Row 2: Slip 1, P 7{11-15}, P2 tog, P1, leave remaining 8 sts unworked; **turn.**

Row 3: Slip 1, K 8{12-16}, SSK, K1; turn.

Row 4: Slip 1, P 9{13-17}, P2 tog, P1; turn.

Row 5: Slip 1, K 10{14-18}, SSK, K1; turn.

Row 6: Slip 1, P 11{15-19}, P2 tog, P1; turn.

Row 7: Slip 1, K 12{16-20}, SSK, K1; turn.

Row 8: Slip 1, P 13{17-21}, P2 tog, P1; turn.

Row 9: Slip 1, K 14{18-22}, SSK, K1; turn.

Row 10: Slip 1, P 15{19-23}, P2 tog, P1: 18{22-26} sts.

GUSSET

The remainder of the sock will be worked in rounds.

Slip the Instep sts from the st holders onto 2 double pointed needles, 14{16-18} sts each.

FOUNDATION ROUND

With **right** side of Heel facing, using an empty double pointed needle and continuing with the working yarn, knit 9{11-13} of the Heel sts.
Place a split-ring marker around the next st to indicate the beginning of the round *(see Markers, page 191).*
Using an empty double pointed needle (this will be needle 1), knit across the remaining 9{11-13} Heel sts. With the same needle, pick up 14{16-18} sts along the side of the Heel Flap *(Fig. 22a, page 199)* and one st in the corner.
With separate needles, knit across the Instep sts (needles 2 and 3).
With an empty needle, pick up one st in the corner and 14{16-18} sts along the side of the Heel Flap. With the same needle, knit 9{11-13} Heel sts.

Stitch count is 24{28-32} sts on the first needle, 14{16-18} sts each on the second and third needles, and 24{28-32} sts on fourth needle for a total of 76{88-100} sts.

GUSSET DECREASES

Rnd 1 (Decrease rnd)**:** Knit across to the last 3 sts on first needle, K2 tog, K1; knit across the second and third needles; on fourth needle, K1, SSK, knit across: 74{86-98} sts.

Rnd 2: Knit around.

Repeat Rnds 1 and 2, 9{11-13} times: 56{64-72} sts, 14{16-18} sts on each needle.

FOOT

Work even knitting each round until Foot measures approximately 7$\frac{1}{2}${8$\frac{1}{2}$-9}"/19{21.5-23} cm from back of Heel **or** 1$\frac{3}{4}${1$\frac{3}{4}$-2$\frac{1}{4}$}"/4.5{4.5-5.5} cm less than total desired Foot length from back of Heel to Toe.

TOE

Rnd 1 (Decrease rnd)**:** Knit across first needle to last 3 sts, K2 tog, K1; on second needle, K1, SSK, knit across; on third needle, knit across to last 3 sts, K2 tog, K1; on fourth needle, K1, SSK, knit across: 4 sts decreased, 52{60-68} sts.

Rnd 2: Knit around.

Repeat Rnds 1 and 2, 7{7-9} times: 24{32-32} sts, 6{8-8} sts on **each** needle.

Using the fourth needle, knit across the sts on the first needle; cut yarn leaving a long end.

Slip the sts from the third needle onto the second needle, so there are 12{16-16} sts on each needle.

Graft remaining stitches together *(Figs. 25a & b, page 200)*.

Repeat for second Sock.

Design by Cathy Hardy.

hannah's ankle socks

In the sweet story Hannah's List, *these socks are made as a friendship gift. They are knitted from the top down with super fine weight yarn—such luxury!*

◼◼◼◻ INTERMEDIATE

Size	Finished Foot Circumference	
Small	7"	(18 cm)
Medium	8"	(20.5 cm)
Large	9"	(23 cm)

Size Note: Instructions are written for size Small with sizes Medium and Large in braces { }. Instructions will be easier to read if you circle all the numbers pertaining to your size. If only one number is given, it applies to all sizes.

MATERIALS

Super Fine Weight Yarn **SUPER FINE 1**
[1.76 ounces, 213 yards
(50 grams, 195 meters) per skein]:
    Main Color - 2 skeins
    Contrasting Color (Cuff) - 1 skein
Set of 5 double pointed knitting needles,
    size 1 (2.25 mm) **or** size needed for gauge
Stitch holders - 2
Split-ring marker
Tapestry needle

GAUGE: In Stockinette Stitch,
        36 sts and 48 rnds = 4" (10 cm)

Techniques used:
• K2 tog (*Fig. 11, page 196*).
• SSK (*Figs. 13a-c, page 196*);
• P2 tog (*Fig. 18, page 198*);

CUFF

Using Contrasting Color, cast on 64{72-80} sts.

Divide sts onto 4 needles (*see Double Pointed Needles, page 193*), placing 16{18-20} sts on each needle.

Note: The Cuff is worked with the **wrong** side facing, since it will be turned down. The yarn end indicates the beginning of the round.

Rnds 1 and 2: (K2, P2) around.

Rnds 3 and 4: Purl around.

Rnds 5 and 6: (P2, K2) around.

Rnds 7 and 8: Purl around.

Repeat Rnds 1-8 until Cuff measures approximately 4" (10 cm) from cast on edge.

Cut Contrasting Color.

Instructions continued on page 130.

LEG

Using Main Color, knit each round until sock measures approximately 7" (18 cm) from cast on edge **or** to desired length.

HEEL FLAP

Dividing Stitches: Knit across first needle; slip sts from the next 2 needles onto 2 separate st holders for Instep to be worked later.

Note: The following pattern will make the Heel dense and will help prevent it from wearing out.

With **wrong** side facing, work Row 1 across both needles onto one needle. The Heel Flap will be worked back and forth across these 32{36-40} sts.

When instructed to slip a stitch, always slip as if to **purl** with yarn held **loosely** to **right** side so that the carried strand shows on the right side forming the woven look.

Row 1: ★ Slip 1, P1; repeat from ★ across.

Row 2: ★ Slip 1, K1; repeat from ★ across.

Rows 3 thru 32{36-40}: Repeat Rows 1 and 2, 15{17-19} times.

TURN HEEL

Begin working in short rows as follows:

Row 1: P 19{21-23}, P2 tog, P1, leave remaining 10{12-14} sts unworked; **turn**.

Row 2: Slip 1, K7, SSK, K1, leave remaining 10{12-14} sts unworked; turn.

Row 3: Slip 1, P8, P2 tog, P1; turn.

Row 4: Slip 1, K9, SSK, K1; turn.

Row 5: Slip 1, P 10, P2 tog, P1; turn.

Row 6: Slip 1, K 11, SSK, K1; turn.

Row 7: Slip 1, P 12, P2 tog, P1; turn.

Row 8: Slip 1, K 13, SSK, K1; turn.

Row 9: Slip 1, P 14, P2 tog, P1; turn.

Row 10: Slip 1, K 15, SSK, K1; turn.

SIZE SMALL ONLY
Row 11: Slip 1, P 16, P2 tog, P1; turn.

Row 12: Slip 1, K 17, SSK, K1: 20 sts.

SIZE MEDIUM ONLY
Row 11: Slip 1, P 16, P2 tog, P1; turn.

Row 12: Slip 1, K 17, SSK, K1; turn.

Row 13: Slip 1, P 18, P2 tog, P1; turn.

Row 14: Slip 1, K 19, SSK, K1: 22 sts.

SIZE LARGE ONLY
Row 11: Slip 1, P 16, P2 tog, P1; turn.

Row 12: Slip 1, K 17, SSK, K1; turn.

Row 13: Slip 1, P 18, P2 tog, P1; turn.

Row 14: Slip 1, K 19, SSK, K1; turn.

Row 15: Slip 1, P 20, P2 tog, P1; turn.

Row 16: Slip 1, K 21, SSK, K1: 24 sts.

GUSSET

The remainder of the sock will be worked in rounds.

Slip the Instep sts from the st holders onto 2 double pointed needles, 16{18-20} sts each.

FOUNDATION ROUND

With **right** side of Heel facing, using the same double pointed needle and continuing with the working yarn, pick up 16{18-20} sts along the side of the Heel Flap *(Fig. 22a, page 199)* and one st in the corner. With separate needles, knit across the Instep sts (needles 2 and 3).
With an empty needle, pick up one st in the corner and 16{18-20} sts along the side of the Heel Flap. With the same needle, knit 10{11-12} Heel sts (this will be needle 4). Place a split-ring marker around the next st to indicate the beginning of the round *(see Markers, page 191)*.

Stitch count is 27{30-33} sts on the first needle, 16{18-20} sts on each of the second and third needles, and 27{30-33} sts on the fourth needle for a total of 86{96-106} sts.

GUSSET DECREASES

Rnd 1 (Decrease rnd): Knit across the first needle to last 3 sts, K2 tog, K1; knit across the second and third needles; on the fourth needle, K1, SSK, knit across: 84{94-104} sts.

Rnd 2: Knit around.

Rnds 3 thru 22{24-26}: Repeat Rnds 1 and 2, 10{11-12} times: total of 64{72-80} sts, 16{18-20} sts on each needle.

FOOT

Work even, knitting each round, until Foot measures approximately 6½{7½-8}"/16.5{19-20.5} cm from back of Heel **or** 1¾{2-2}"/4.5{5-5} cm less than total desired Foot length from back of Heel to Toe.

TOE

Rnd 1 (Decrease rnd): Knit across first needle to last 3 sts, K2 tog, K1; on second needle, K1, SSK, knit across; on third needle, knit across to last 3 sts, K2 tog, K1; on fourth needle, K1, SSK, knit across: 15{17-19} sts on each needle.

Rnd 2: Knit around.

Rnds 3 thru 20{24-24}: Repeat Rnds 1 and 2, 9{11-11} times: 6{6-8} sts on each needle.

Using the fourth needle, knit across the sts on the first needle; cut yarn leaving a long end for grafting.

Slip the stitches from the third needle onto the second needle, so there are 12{12-16} sts on each of two needles.

Graft the remaining sts together *(Figs. 25a & b, page 200)*.

Repeat for second Sock.

Design by Cathy Hardy.

thick socks

When little feet need extra warmth, these socks are the ones to knit! They're from A Charity Guide for Knitters. A soft, medium weight yarn makes them so cozy to wear!

Children Size	Finished Foot Circumference	
Small	5"	(12.5 cm)
Medium	6"	(15 cm)
Large	6³/₄"	(17 cm)
X-Large	7¹/₂"	(19 cm)

Size Note: Instructions are written for size Small with sizes Medium, Large, and X-Large in braces { }. Instructions will be easier to read if you circle all the numbers pertaining to your child's size. If only one number is given, it applies to all sizes.

MATERIALS

Medium Weight Yarn
[3.5 ounces, 220 yards
(100 grams, 201 meters) per hank]:
 1 hank
Two 16" (40.5 cm) Circular knitting needles, size 5 (3.75 mm) **or** size needed for gauge
Yarn needle

GAUGE: In Stockinette Stitch,
 19 sts = 4" (10 cm)

Techniques used:

- K2 tog *(Fig. 11, page 196)*
- SSK *(Figs.. 13a-c, page 196)*
- P2 tog *(Fig. 18, page 198)*

CUFF

Cast on 24{28-32-36} sts on one circular needle.

Slip the last 12{14-16-18} sts onto the second circular needle, placing them at the center of the cable *(Figs. 1b-d, page 192)*.

Note: The yarn end indicates the beginning of the round.

Work in K1, P1 ribbing for 1{1-1¹/₂-2}"/2.5{2.5-4-5} cm.

LEG

When instructed to slip a stitch, always slip as if to **purl** with yarn held loosely to **wrong** side.

Rnd 1: ★ Slip 1, K1; repeat from ★ around.

Rnd 2: Knit around.

Repeat Rnds 1 and 2 until Sock measures approximately 3¹/₂{4¹/₂-5¹/₂-6}"/9{11.5-14-15} cm from cast on edge, ending by working Rnd 2.

Instructions continued on page 134.

HEEL FLAP

Begin working in rows on the first needle only. The stitches on the second needle won't be used until the Gusset.

Note: The following pattern will make the Heel dense and will help prevent it from wearing out.

Row 1: ★ Slip 1, K1; repeat from ★ across.

Row 2: ★ Slip 1, P1; repeat from ★ across.

Repeat Rows 1 and 2, 4{5-5-6} times.

TURN HEEL

Begin working in short rows as follows:

Row 1: Slip 1, K6{7-8-9}, SSK, K1, leave remaining 2{3-4-5} sts unworked; **turn.**

Row 2: Slip 1, P3, P2 tog, P1, leave remaining 2{3-4-5} sts unworked; **turn.**

Row 3: Slip 1, K4, SSK, K1; turn.

Row 4: Slip 1, P5, P2 tog, P1; turn.

SIZE MEDIUM ONLY

Row 5: Slip 1, K6, SSK.

Row 6: Slip 1, P6, P2 tog: 8 sts.

SIZE LARGE ONLY

Row 5: Slip 1, K6, SSK, K1.

Row 6: Slip 1, P7, P2 tog, P1: 10 sts.

SIZE X-LARGE ONLY

Row 5: Slip 1, K6, SSK, K1; turn.

Row 6: Slip 1, P7, P2 tog, P1; turn.

Row 7: Slip 1, K8, SSK.

Row 8: Slip 1, P8, P2 tog: 10 sts.

GUSSET

Begin working with two circular needles in the round.

Rnd 1: Still using first needle, knit across the Heel sts, pick up 5{6-6-7} sts working in the end of rows along side of Heel Flap *(Fig. 22a, page 199)*; with the second needle, (slip 1, K1) across the Leg.

Rnd 2: Using first needle, pick up 5{6-6-7} sts in the end of rows along second side of Heel Flap, knit to end of needle; knit across second needle: 18{20-22-24} sts on the first needle and 12{14-16-18} sts on the second needle.

Rnd 3: K1, SSK, knit across first needle to last 3 sts, K2 tog, K1; (slip 1, K1) across second needle: 16{18-20-22} sts on first needle.

Rnd 4: Knit around.

Repeat Rnds 3 and 4 twice: 12{14-16-18} sts on **each** needle.

FOOT

Rnd 1: Knit across first needle; (slip 1, K1) across second needle.

Rnd 2: Knit around.

Repeat Rnds 1 and 2 until Foot measures approximately 4{4-4³/₄-6³/₄}"/10{10-12-17} cm from back of Heel, ending by working Rnd 2.

TOE

Rnd 1 (Decrease rnd)**:** K1, SSK, knit across first needle to last 3 sts, K2 tog, K1; with the second needle, K1, SSK, work across in pattern to last 3 sts, K2 tog, K1: 10{12-14-16} sts on **each** needle.

Rnd 2: Knit around.

Repeat Rnds 1 and 2, 2{2-3-4} times: 6{8-8-8} sts on **each** needle.

Cut yarn leaving a long end.

Graft remaining stitches together *(Figs. 25a & b, page 200)*.

Repeat for second Sock.

Design by Cathy Hardy.

ribbed turtleneck

This trendy turtleneck is from Debbie's Favorites, because as Debbie says,
"To me, the look of grey and khaki together is a fashion classic, and my friend Lisa Ellis's
soft pullover with tortoiseshell trim is one of my weekend favorites."

■■■□ INTERMEDIATE

Size	Finished Chest Measurement
Small	36" (91.5 cm)
Medium	38¹/₄" (97 cm)
Large	40¹/₂" (103 cm)

Size Note: Instructions are written for size Small with sizes Medium and Large in braces { }. Instructions will be easier to read if you circle all the numbers pertaining to your size. If only one number is given, it applies to all sizes.

MATERIALS
Bulky Weight Yarn **5**
[3¹/₂ ounces, 110 yards
(100 grams, 126 meters) per skein]:
    8{9-9} skeins
Bulky Weight Novelty Yarn
[1³/₄ ounces, 66 yards
(50 grams, 60 meters) per ball]:
    1{2-2} ball(s)
Straight knitting needles, size 10 (6 mm) **or**
    size needed for gauge
16" (40.5 cm) Circular knitting needle,
    size 10 (6 mm)
Double pointed knitting needles,
    size 10 (6 mm) (for 3-Needle Bind Off)
Stitch holders - 5
Marker
Yarn needle

GAUGE: In pattern with Bulky Weight Yarn, 14 sts and 20 rows = 4" (10 cm)

Techniques used:
• increasing evenly *(page 195)*
• knit increase *(Figs. 7a & b, page 195)*
• K2 tog *(Fig. 11, page 196)*
• SSK *(Figs. 13a-c, page 196)*

BACK
BOTTOM BAND
With straight knitting needles and Novelty Yarn, cast on 50{54-58} sts.

Row 1: Knit across.

Row 2 (Right side): Purl across.

Repeat Rows 1 and 2 for 2" (5 cm), ending by working Row 1 and increasing 15 sts evenly spaced across; cut yarn: 65{69-73} sts.

Instructions continued on page 138.

BODY
Change to Bulky Weight Yarn.

Row 1 (Right side): K2, P1, (K3, P1) across to last 2 sts, K2.

Row 2: P1, (K3, P1) across.

Repeat Rows 1 and 2 for pattern, until piece measures approximately 14½{14½-15}"/37{37-38} cm from cast on edge, ending by working Row 2.

ARMHOLE SHAPING
Maintain established pattern throughout.

Rows 1 and 2: Bind off 4{4-5} sts at the beginning of the next 2 rows, work across: 57{61-63} sts.

Bind off one st at the beginning of the next 6{6-8} rows, work across: 51{55-55} sts.

Work even until Armholes measure approximately 8½{9-9}"/21.5{23-23} cm, ending by working a **right** side row.

NECK SHAPING
Both sides of the Neck are worked at the same time, using separate yarn for **each** side. Maintain established pattern throughout.

Row 1: Work across 15{16-16} sts, slip next 21{23-23} sts onto first st holder; with second yarn, work across: 15{16-16} sts **each** side.

Row 2 (Right side): Work across to within 2 sts of Neck edge, K2 tog; with second yarn, SSK, work across: 14{15-15} sts **each** side.

Row 3: Work across; with second yarn, work across.

Place sts from each shoulder onto st holders for 3-Needle Bind Off.

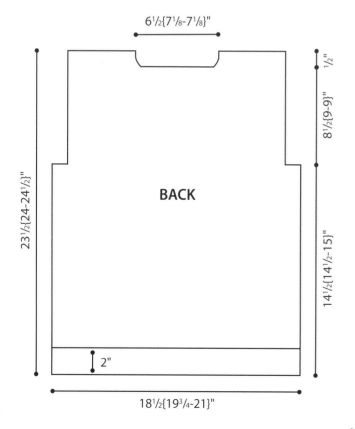

BACK

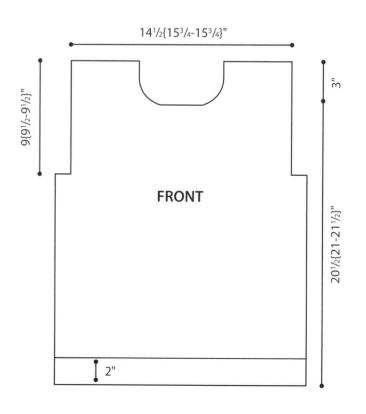

FRONT

Note: Turtleneck includes two edge stitches.

FRONT

Work same as Back until Front measures approximately 20½{21-21½}"/52{53.5-54.5} cm, ending by working a **right** side row: 51{55-55} sts.

NECK SHAPING

Row 1: Work across 19{20-20} sts, bind off next 13{15-15} sts, work across: 19{20-20} sts **each** side.

Both sides of the Neck are worked at the same time, using separate yarn for **each** side. Maintain established pattern throughout.

Row 2 (Right side): Work across to within 2 sts of Neck edge, K2 tog; with second yarn, SSK, knit across: 18{19-19} sts **each** side.

Row 3: Work across; with second yarn, work across.

Row 4 (Decrease row): Work across to within 2 sts of Neck edge, K2 tog; with second yarn, SSK, work across: 17{18-18} sts **each** side.

Rows 5-10: Repeat Rows 3 and 4, 3 times: 14{15-15} sts **each** side.

Work even until Front measures same as Back to shoulders, ending by working a **wrong** side row.

Place sts from each shoulder onto st holders for 3-Needle Bind Off.

SLEEVE (Make 2)
BOTTOM BAND
With straight knitting needles and Novelty Yarn, cast on 22{24-24} sts.

Row 1: Knit across.

Row 2 (Right side): Purl across.

Repeat Rows 1 and 2 for 2" (5 cm), ending by working Row 2 and increasing 7{9-9} sts evenly spaced across; cut yarn: 29{33-33} sts.

BODY
Change to Bulky Weight Yarn.

Row 1: P1, (K3, P1) across.

Row 2 (Right side): K2, P1, (K3, P1) across to last 2 sts, K2.

Row 3: P1, (K3, P1) across.

Row 4 (Increase row): K1, increase in next st, P1, (K3, P1) across to last 2 sts, increase in next st, K1: 31{35-35} sts.

Working new stitches in pattern, continue to increase one stitch at **each** edge in same manner, every fourth row, 15 times: 61{65-65} sts.

Work even until Sleeve measures approximately 17½{17½-18}"/44.5{44.5-45.5} cm from cast on edge, ending by working a **wrong** side row.

SLEEVE CAP
Maintain established pattern throughout.

Rows 1 and 2: Bind off 4{4-5} sts at the beginning of the next 2 rows, work across: 53{57-55} sts.

Row 3: SSK, work across to last 2 sts, K2 tog: 51{55-53} sts.

Instructions continued on page 140.

Row 4: Work across.

Row 5: SSK, work across to last 2 sts, K2 tog: 49{53-51} sts.

Continue to decrease one stitch at **each** edge, every other row, 1{1-2} time(s) **more**; then decrease every row, 13{14-12} times: 21{23-23} sts.

Bind off 2 sts at the beginning of the next 4 rows, work across: 13{15-15} sts.

Bind off remaining sts in pattern.

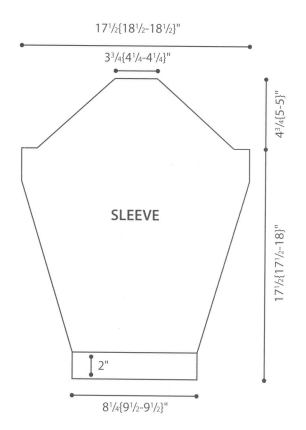

17½{18½-18½}"

3¾{4¼-4¼}"

4¾{5-5}"

SLEEVE

17½{17½-18}"

2"

8¼{9½-9½}"

FINISHING

Slip sts from Front and Back right shoulder st holders onto double pointed knitting needles.
Work 3-Needle Bind Off *(Fig. 26, page 200)*.

Repeat for left shoulder.

TURTLENECK

With **right** side facing, using Bulky Weight Yarn and circular knitting needle, and beginning at left shoulder seam, pick up 11 sts evenly spaced along left Neck edge *(Figs. 22a & b, page 199)*, pick up 13{16-16} sts across front Neck bound off sts, pick up 11 sts evenly spaced along right Neck edge to shoulder seam, pick up 2{1-1} st(s) along right back Neck edge, knit 21{23-23} sts from Back st holder, pick up 2 sts along left back Neck edge; place a marker to mark the beginning of the rnd *(see Markers, page 191)*: 60{64-64} sts.

Rnd 1: (K2, P2) around.

Repeat Rnd 1 until Turtleneck measures approximately 4" (10 cm).

Bind off all sts **very loosely**.

Matching center of Sleeve Cap with shoulder seam, sew Sleeves into Armhole opening with Bulky Weight Yarn.

With Bulky Weight Yarn, weave underarm and sides in one continuous seam *(Fig. 23, page 199)*.

Designed by Lisa Ellis.

leif's sweater

This boy's sweater is wonderfuly textured! It can be knit in small, medium, or large sizes. It comes from Knit Along with Debbie Macomber—The Cedar Cove Collection, *which has thirteen patterns to knit and four delicious recipes to enjoy. Charlotte Jefferson would love to make this sweater for her great-grandson Leif. And of course, she already has the recipes!*

Shown on page 143.

◼◼◼◻ INTERMEDIATE

Size	Actual Chest Measurement	Finished Chest Measurement
Small	22-24¹/₂"/56-62 cm	26¹/₂" (67.5 cm)
Medium	25-27"/63.5-68.5 cm	29" (73.5 cm)
Large	27¹/₂-29"/70-73.5 cm	31¹/₄" (79.5 cm)

Size Note: Instructions are written for size Small, with sizes Medium and Large in braces { }. Instructions will be easier to read if you circle all the numbers pertaining to your child's size. If only one number is given, it applies to all sizes.

MATERIALS

Light Weight Superwash Wool Yarn [LIGHT 3]
   [4 ounces, 240 yards
   (113 grams, 220 meters) per hank]:
     3{3-4} hanks
Two 29" (73.5 cm) Circular knitting needles,
   size 6 (4 mm) **or** size needed for gauge
Note: A pair of straight knitting needles can be substituted for one of the circular knitting needles which is used to work the 3-needle bind off.
16" (40.5 cm) Circular knitting needle,
   size 4 (3.5 mm)
Stitch holders - 2
Marker
Yarn needle

GAUGE: With larger size needles,
   in Seed Stitch, 20 sts = 4" (10 cm);
   in Basket Weave,
   5 repeats (30 sts) = 6" (15.25 cm);
   24 rows = 3" (7.5 cm)

Tip: Do not hesitate to change needle size to obtain correct gauge.

Techniques used:
• knit increase *(Figs. 7a & b, page 195)*
• increasing evenly *(page 195)*
• decreases *(pages 196-198)*

Instructions continued on page 142.

BACK
RIBBING

With smaller size needle, cast on 66{74-78} sts.

Row 1: P2, (K2, P2) across.

Row 2: K2, (P2, K2) across.

Repeat Rows 1 and 2 for 1$\frac{1}{2}${2-2}"/4{5-5} cm, ending by working Row 1 and increasing 1{0-1} st(s) at **each** edge of last row *(see Zeros, page 191)*: 68{74-80} sts.

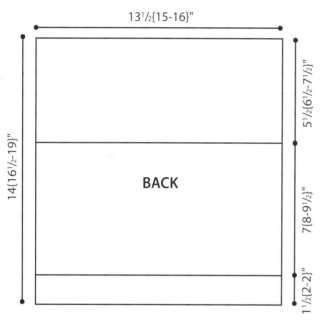

13$\frac{1}{2}${15-16}"

14{16$\frac{1}{2}$-19}"

5$\frac{1}{2}${6$\frac{1}{2}$-7$\frac{1}{2}$}"

7{8-9$\frac{1}{2}$}"

1$\frac{1}{2}${2-2}"

BACK

Note: Sweater includes two edge stitches.

BODY

Change to larger size needles.

Row 1 (Right side): Knit across.

Row 2: P3, K4, (P2, K4) across to last st, P1.

Rows 3 and 4: Repeat Rows 1 and 2.

Row 5: Knit across.

Row 6: (K4, P2) across to last 2 sts, K2.

Rows 7 and 8: Repeat Rows 5 and 6.

Repeat Rows 1-8 for Basket Weave until Back measures approximately 8$\frac{1}{2}${10-11$\frac{1}{2}$}"/21.5{25.5-29} cm from cast on edge, ending by working Row 4 or Row 8.

YOKE

Rows 1 and 2: Knit across.

Rows 3 and 4: Purl across.

Rows 5-8: Repeat Rows 1-4.

Row 9: (K1, P1) across.

Row 10: (P1, K1) across.

Repeat Rows 9 and 10 for Seed Stitch until Yoke measures approximately 5$\frac{1}{2}${6$\frac{1}{2}$-7$\frac{1}{2}$}"/ 14{16.5-19} cm, ending by working a **wrong** side row; cut yarn.

Leave stitches on the circular needle and set Back aside.

FRONT

Work same as Back until Yoke measures approximately 4{4$\frac{1}{2}$-5}"/10{11.5-12.5} cm, ending by working a **wrong** side row: 68{74-80} sts.

NECK SHAPING

Both sides of Neck are worked at the same time, using a separate yarn for **each** side. Maintain established pattern throughout.

Row 1: Work across 23{26-28} sts, slip next 22{22-24} sts onto st holder; with second yarn, work across: 23{26-28} sts **each** side.

Instructions continued on page 144.

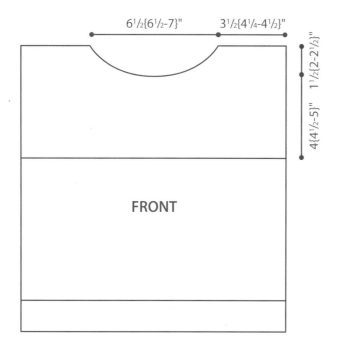

6¹/₂{6¹/₂-7}" 3¹/₂{4¹/₄-4¹/₂}"

1¹/₂{2-2¹/₂}"

4{4¹/₂-5}"

FRONT

Work even until Front measures same as Back, ending by working a **wrong** side row.

Join Front to Back at Left shoulder using the 3-needle bind off method as follows: Holding pieces with **right** sides together and needles parallel to each other, insert a third needle as if to **knit** into the first st on the front needle **and** into the first st on the back needle (*Fig. A*). Knit these 2 sts tog and slip them off the needle, ★ knit the next st on each needle tog and slip them off the needle. To bind off, insert the left needle into the first st on the right needle and pull the first st over the second st and off the right needle; repeat from ★ across until all of the sts on the shoulder have been bound off.

Fig. A

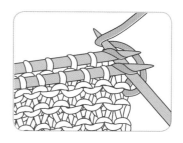

Slip 32{32-34} sts from Back onto st holder for neck. Join Front to Back at Right shoulder using the 3-needle bind off method.

Row 2 (Decrease row)**:** Work across to within 2 sts of neck edge, decrease; with second yarn, decrease, work across: 22{25-27} sts **each** side.

Row 3: Work across; with second yarn, work across.

Rows 4-10: Repeat Rows 2 and 3, 3 times; then repeat Row 2 once **more**: 18{21-23} sts **each** side.

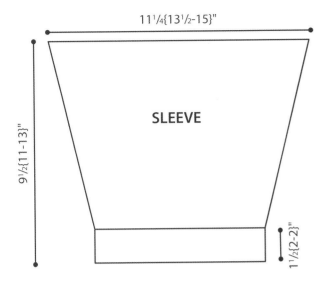

11¼{13½-15}"

9½{11-13}"

SLEEVE

1½{2-2}"

Beginning with Row 2, work in Basket Weave same as Back, increasing one stitch at **each** edge, every 8{6-6} rows, 6{9-12} times: 56{68-74} sts.

Work even until Sleeve measures approximately 9½{11-13}"/24{28-33} cm from cast on edge **or to desired length**, ending by working a **wrong** side row.

Bind off all sts in pattern.

FINISHING

Sew Sleeves to sweater, placing center of Sleeve at shoulder seam and beginning between Garter ridge (Rows 4 and 5) at beginning of Yoke.

Weave underarm and side in one continuous seam (*Fig. 23, page 199*).

NECK RIBBING

With **right** side facing, slip 32{32-34} sts from Back st holder onto smaller size needle and knit across, pick up 11{15-19} sts evenly spaced along left Front neck edge (*Fig. 22a, page 199*), slip 22{22-24} sts from Front st holder onto second end of circular needle and knit across, pick up 11{15-19} sts evenly spaced along right Front neck edge, place marker to indicate beginning of round (*see Markers, page 191*): 76{84-96} sts.

Work in K2, P2 ribbing for 1½" (4 cm).

Bind off all sts **loosely** in established ribbing.

Design by Terri Fahrenholtz.

SLEEVE (Make 2)
RIBBING
With smaller size needle, cast on 38{42-42} sts **loosely.**

Row 1: P2, (K2, P2) across.

Row 2: K2, (P2, K2) across.

Repeat Rows 1 and 2 for 1½{2-2}"/4{5-5} cm, ending by working Row 1.

BODY
Change to larger size needles.

Row 1 (Right side): Knit across increasing 6{8-8} sts evenly spaced: 44{50-50} sts.

jolene's pullover

Rachel Pendergast is a manicurist who works at the Get Nailed salon in Cedar Cove. Rachel doesn't knit, but she promised one of her clients a series of free manicures if she would knit this sweater for Jolene Peyton. Jolene is a sweet nine-year-old who lives with her widowed dad and wishes Rachel would become her new mom.

■■■□ **INTERMEDIATE**

Size	Actual Chest Measurement	Finished Chest Measurement
Small	26-28"/66-71 cm	30½" (77.5 cm)
Medium	29-31"/73.5-78.5 cm	33¼" (84.5 cm)
Large	32-34"/81.5-86.5 cm	36" (91.5 cm)

Size Note: Instructions are written for size Small, with sizes Medium and Large in braces { }. Instructions will be easier to read if you circle all the numbers pertaining to your child's size. If only one number is given, it applies to all sizes.

MATERIALS

Medium Weight Yarn (**LIGHT 3**)
[6 ounces, 315 yards
(170 grams, 288 meters) per skein]:
   3 skeins
Straight knitting needles, sizes 7 (4.5 mm)
   and 9 (5.5 mm) **or** sizes needed for gauge
16" (40.5 cm) Circular knitting needle,
   size 7 (4.5 mm)
Cable needle
Stitch holders - 2
Marker
Yarn needle

GAUGE: With larger size needles, in Stockinette Stitch, 18 sts and 24 rows = 4" (10 cm)

Tip: Do not hesitate to change needle size to obtain correct gauge.

Techniques used:
- knit increase *(Figs. 7a & b, page 195)*
- purl increase *(Fig. 9, page 195)*
- K2 tog *(Fig. 11, page 196)*
- SSK *(Figs. 13a-c, page 196)*
- P2 tog *(Fig. 18, page 198)*
- P2 tog tbl *(Fig. 19, page 198)*

STITCH GUIDE

BACK CABLE (uses 4 sts)
Slip next 2 sts onto cable needle and hold in **back** of work, K2 from left needle, K2 from cable needle.

FRONT CABLE (uses 4 sts)
Slip next 2 sts onto cable needle and hold in **front** of work, K2 from left needle, K2 from cable needle.

Instructions continued on page 148.

BACK

RIBBING

With smaller size needles, cast on 70{76-82} sts.

Work in K1, P1 ribbing for 2" (5 cm) increasing one st at end of last row: 71{77-83} sts.

BODY

Change to larger size needles.

Row 1 (Right side)**:** Knit across.

Row 2: Purl across.

Row 3: K2, P1, (K5, P1) across to last 2 sts, K2.

Row 4: (P1, K1) twice, P3, (K1, P1, K1, P3) across to last 4 sts, (K1, P1) twice.

Row 5: K4, P1, K1, P1, (K3, P1, K1, P1) across to last 4 sts, K4.

Row 6: P5, (K1, P5) across.

Row 7: Knit across.

Row 8: Purl across.

Rows 9-11: Knit across.

Row 12: P2, K1, (P5, K1) across to last 2 sts, P2.

Note: Pullover includes two edge stitches.

Rows 13 and 14: Repeat Rows 11 and 12.

Rows 15-17: Knit across.

Repeat Rows 2-17 until Back measures approximately 11½{12½-14}"/29{32-35.5} cm from cast on edge, ending by working Row 8 or Row 14.

YOKE & ARMHOLE SHAPING

Rows 1 and 2: Bind off 4 sts, knit across: 63{69-75} sts.

Row 3: K 31{34-37}, knit into front **and** back of next st, knit across: 64{70-76} sts.

Row 4: Knit across.

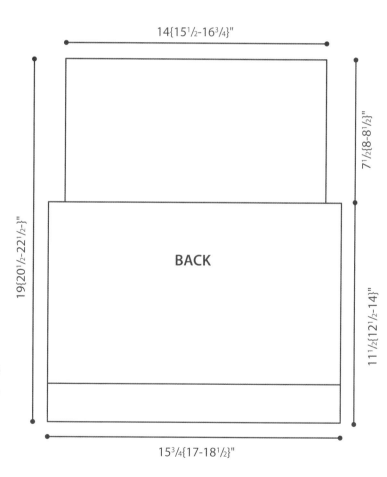

14{15½-16¾}"

7½{8-8½}"

BACK

19{20½-22½-}"

11½{12½-14}"

15¾{17-18½}"

Row 5: K8{10-12}, P1, K1, P1, K2, back cable, P1, K1, P1, ★ K6{7-8}, P1, K1, P1, K2, back cable, P1, K1, P1; repeat from ★ once **more**, K8{10-12}.

Row 6: P9{11-13}, K1, P8, K1, ★ P8{9-10}, K1, P8, K1; repeat from ★ once **more**, P9{11-13}.

Row 7: K8{10-12}, P1, K1, P1, front cable, K2, P1, K1, P1, ★ K6{7-8}, P1, K1, P1, front cable, K2, P1, K1, P1; repeat from ★ once **more**, K8{10-12}.

Row 8: P9{11-13}, K1, P8, K1, ★ P8{9-10}, K1, P8, K1; repeat from ★ once **more**, P9{11-13}.

Repeat Rows 5-8 until Yoke measures approximately 7¹⁄₂{8-8¹⁄₂}"/19{20.5-21.5} cm, ending by working a **wrong** side row.

Bind off 21{23-25} sts, work across in established pattern until 22{24-26} sts are on right needle, then slip them onto st holder; bind off remaining sts; cut yarn.

FRONT

Work same as Back until Yoke measures approximately 5{5¹⁄₂-5¹⁄₂}"/12.5{14-14} cm, ending by working a **wrong** side row: 64{70-76} sts.

NECK SHAPING

Both sides of Neck are worked at the same time, using a separate yarn for **each** side. Maintain established pattern throughout.

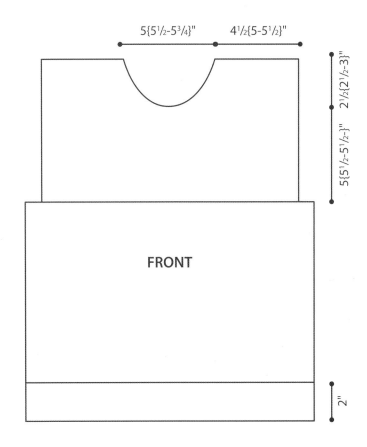

Row 1: Work across 24{27-29} sts, K2 tog , slip next 12{12-14} sts onto st holder; with second yarn, SSK, work across: 25{28-30} sts **each** side.

Row 2 (Decrease row): Work across to within 2 sts of neck edge, P2 tog through back loops; with second yarn, P2 tog, work across: 24{27-29} sts **each** side.

Row 3 (Decrease row): Work across to within 2 sts of neck edge, K2 tog; with second yarn, SSK, work across: 23{26-28} sts **each** side.

Instructions continued on page 150.

Row 4: Work across; with second yarn, work across.

Repeat Rows 3 and 4, 1{2-2} time(s); then repeat Row 3 once **more**: 21{23-25} sts **each** side.

Work even until Front measures same as Back, ending by working a **wrong** side row.

Bind off remaining sts.

Sew shoulder seams.

SLEEVE

With **right** side facing and using larger size needles, pick up 68{72-76} sts evenly spaced across Front and Back Yoke (*Fig. 22a, page 199*).

Row 1: P7{7-8}, K1, P8, K1, ★ P 12{14-15}, K1, P8, K1; repeat from ★ once **more**, P7{7-8}.

Row 2: K6{6-7}, P1, K1, P1, front cable, K2, P1, K1, P1, ★ K 10{12-13}, P1, K1, P1, front cable, K2, P1, K1, P1; repeat from ★ once **more**, K6{6-7}.

Row 3: P7{7-8}, K1, P8, K1, ★ P 12{14-15}, K1, P8, K1; repeat from ★ once **more**, P7{7-8}.

Row 4: K6{6-7}, P1, K1, P1, K2, back cable, P1, K1, P1, ★ K 10{12-13}, P1, K1, P1, K2, back cable, P1, K1, P1; repeat from ★ once **more**, K6{6-7}.

Rows 5-13: Repeat Rows 1-4 twice, then repeat Row 1 once **more**.

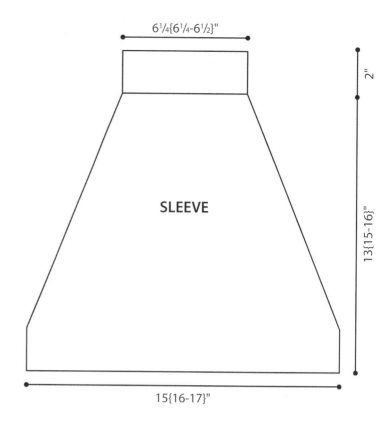

SLEEVE

6¼{6¼-6½}"

2"

13{15-16}"

15{16-17}"

Row 14 (Decrease row): K1, SSK, K3{3-4}, P1, K1, P1, front cable, K2, P1, K1, P1, ★ K 10{12-13}, P1, K1, P1, front cable, K2, P1, K1, P1; repeat from ★ once **more**, K3{3-4}, K2 tog, K1: 66{70-74} sts.

Row 15: P6{6-7}, K1, P8, K1, ★ P 12{14-15}, K1, P8, K1; repeat from ★ once **more**, P6{6-7}.

Row 16: K5{5-6}, P1, K1, P1, K2, back cable, P1, K1, P1, ★ K 10{12-13}, P1, K1, P1, K2, back cable, P1, K1, P1; repeat from ★ once **more**, K5{5-6}.

Row 17: P6{6-7}, K1, P8, K1, ★ P 12{14-15}, K1, P8, K1; repeat from ★ once **more**, P6{6-7}.

Row 18 (Decrease row): K1, SSK, K2{2-3}, P1, K1, P1, front cable, K2, P1, K1, P1, ★ K 10{12-13}, P1, K1, P1, front cable, K2, P1, K1, P1; repeat from ★ once **more**, K2{2-3}, K2 tog, K1: 64{68-72} sts.

Row 19: P5{5-6}, K1, P8, K1, ★ P 12{14-15}, K1, P8, K1; repeat from ★ once **more**, P5{5-6}.

Row 20: K4{4-5}, P1, K1, P1, K2, back cable, P1, K1, P1, ★ K 10{12-13}, P1, K1, P1, K2, back cable, P1, K1, P1; repeat from ★ once **more**, K4{4-5}.

Row 21: P5{5-6}, K1, P8, K1, ★ P 12{14-15}, K1, P8, K1; repeat from ★ once **more**, P5{5-6}.

Row 22 (Decrease row): K1, SSK, K1{1-2}, P1, K1, P1, front cable, K2, P1, K1, P1, ★ K 10{12-13}, P1, K1, P1, front cable, K2, P1, K1, P1; repeat from ★ once **more**, K1{1-2}, K2 tog, K1: 62{66-70} sts.

Row 23: P4{4-5}, K1, P8, K1, ★ P 12{14-15}, K1, P8, K1; repeat from ★ once **more**, P4{4-5}.

Row 24: K3{3-4}, P1, K1, P1, K2, back cable, P1, K1, P1, ★ K 10{12-13}, P1, K1, P1, K2, back cable, P1, K1, P1; repeat from ★ once **more**, K3{3-4}.

Row 25: P4{4-5}, K1, P8, K1, ★ P 12{14-15}, K1, P8, K1; repeat from ★ once **more**, P4{4-5}.

Row 26 (Decrease row): K1, SSK, knit across to last 3 sts, K2 tog, K1: 60{64-68} sts.

Rows 27-29: Knit across.

Row 30 (Decrease row): K1, SSK, knit across to last 3 sts, K2 tog, K1: 58{62-66} sts.

Row 31: Purl across.

Row 32: K5{4-6}, P1, (K5, P1) across to last 4{3-5} sts, knit across.

Row 33: P3{2-4}, K1, P1, K1, (P3, K1, P1, K1) across to last 4{3-5} sts, purl across.

Row 34 (Decrease row): K1, SSK, K 0{0-1} *(see Zeros, page 191)*, P1{0-1}, (K3, P1, K1, P1) across to last 6{5-7} sts, K3{2-3}, P 0{0-1}, K2 tog, K1: 56{60-64} sts.

Row 35: P6{5-7}, K1, (P5, K1) across to last 1{6-2} sts, purl across.

Row 36: Knit across.

Row 37: Purl across.

Row 38 (Decrease row): K1, SSK, knit across to last 3 sts, K2 tog, K1: 54{58-62} sts.

Instructions continued on page 152.

Rows 39 and 40: Knit across.

Row 41: P2{1-3}, K1, (P5, K1) across to last 3{2-4} sts, purl across.

Row 42 (Decrease row): K1, SSK, knit across to last 3 sts, K2 tog, K1: 52{56-60} sts.

Row 43: P1{6-2}, K1, (P5, K1) across to last 2{1-3} sts, purl across.

Rows 44 and 45: Knit across.

Row 46 (Decrease row): K1, SSK, knit across to last 3 sts, K2 tog, K1: 50{54-58} sts.

Working in pattern, continue to decrease one stitch at **each** edge in same manner, every fourth row, 6{9-10} times **more**: 38{36-38} sts.

Work even until Sleeve measures approximately 13{15-16}"/33{38-40.5} cm, ending by working a **wrong** side row.

RIBBING
Change to smaller size needles.

Row 1: Work in K1, P1 ribbing across decreasing 10{8-8} sts evenly spaced: 28{28-30} sts.

Work in established ribbing for 2" (5 cm), ending by working a **wrong** side row.

Bind off all sts **loosely** in ribbing.

Repeat for second Sleeve.

FINISHING
Weave underarm and side in one continuous seam *(Fig. 23, page 199)*.

NECK BAND
With **right** side facing and using circular needle, knit 22{24-26} sts from Back st holder, pick up 15{15-18} sts along left Front neck edge, slip 12{12-14} sts from Front st holder onto second end of circular needle and knit across, pick up 15{15-18} sts along right Front neck edge, place marker to indicate beginning of round *(see Markers, page 191)*: 64{66-76} sts.

Work in K1, P1 ribbing for 2" (5 cm).

Bind off all sts **very loosely** in established ribbing.

Fold Neck Band in half to **wrong** side of sweater and sew loosely in place along base of ribbing.

Design by Joan Beebe.

baxter's cozy coat

Anne Marie Roche of Twenty Wishes *has a morning routine while living in the tiny apartment above her bookstore. She walks Baxter, her Yorkshire terrier, along Blossom Street and around a nearby park. Now that she's learning how to knit, she plans to make him a new coat to wear for these excursions. With six sizes to choose from, you can make this coat to fit a little canine like Baxter, or any lucky dog up to size XX-Large!*

Shown on page 155.

◖■■▢▢ **EASY**

Size	Chest Measurement
X-Small	12" (30.5 cm)
Small	16" (40.5 cm)
Medium	20" (51 cm)
Large	24" (61 cm)
X-Large	28" (71 cm)
XX-Large	32" (81.5 cm)

Size Note: Instructions are written for sizes X-Small, Small, and Medium in the first set of braces { }, with sizes Large, X-Large and XX-Large in the second set of braces. Instructions will be easier to read if you circle all the numbers pertaining to your dog's size. If only one number is given, it applies to all sizes.

MATERIALS

Medium Weight Yarn
[3.5 ounces, 170 yards
(100 grams, 156 meters) per skein]:
   {1-1-2}{2-2-3} skein(s)
Straight knitting needles, sizes 7 (4.5 mm)
   and 9 (5.5 mm) **or** sizes needed for gauge
Yarn needle
³/₄" (19 mm) Buttons - {1-1-1}{2-2-2}

GAUGE: With larger size needles, in pattern,
   16 sts and 26 rows = 4" (10 cm)

Techniques used:

- YO (*Fig. 5a, page 194*)
- knit increase (*Figs. 7a & b, page 195*)
- K2 tog (*Fig. 11, page 196*)
- P2 tog (*Fig. 18, page 198*)

BODY

With larger size needles,
cast on {27-37-47}{57-67-77} sts.

Rows 1-5: Knit across.

Row 6: K5, ★ P2 tog without slipping sts off needle, then knit same 2 sts together; repeat from ★ across to last 4 sts, K4.

Row 7 (Right side): Knit across.

Row 8: K4, ★ P2 tog without slipping sts off needle, then knit same 2 sts together; repeat from ★ across to last 5 sts, K5.

Instructions continued on page 154.

Row 9: Knit across.

Repeat Rows 6-9 for pattern until Body measures approximately {6$\frac{1}{4}$-8$\frac{3}{4}$-11$\frac{1}{2}$}{13$\frac{1}{2}$-15$\frac{1}{2}$-17$\frac{1}{2}$}"/{16-22-29}{34.5-39.5-44.5} cm from cast on edge **or** to within {1$\frac{1}{4}$-1$\frac{1}{4}$-1$\frac{1}{2}$}{1$\frac{1}{2}$-1$\frac{1}{2}$-1$\frac{1}{2}$}"/{3-3-4}{4-4-4} cm of desired length to base of neck.

NECK SHAPING

Continue working in pattern, increasing one stitch at each edge, every other row, {4-4-5}{5-5-5} times, knitting new stitches: {35-45-57}{67-77-87} sts.

NECK RIBBING

Change to smaller size needles.

Work in K1, P1 ribbing for {3-4-4}{5-5-6}"/{7.5-10-10}{12.5-12.5-15} cm.

Bind off all sts **loosely** in ribbing.

BAND

With smaller size needles,
cast on {7-9-11}{15-17-19} sts.

Knit 4 rows.

SIZES X-SMALL, SMALL AND MEDIUM ONLY
Buttonhole Row: K{2-3-4}, K2 tog, YO, knit across.

SIZES LARGE, X-LARGE AND XX-LARGE ONLY
Buttonhole Row: K2, K2 tog, YO, K{6-8-10}, K2 tog, YO, K3.

Knit every row until Band measures approximately {5-6$\frac{1}{2}$-8}{9$\frac{1}{2}$-11-12$\frac{1}{2}$}"/{12.5-16.5-20.5}{24-28-32} cm from cast on edge **or** to desired length.

Bind off all sts leaving a long end for sewing.

FINISHING

Place the Coat on your dog and mark placement for Band. Sew Band in place.

Sew button(s) to Coat to correspond with buttonhole(s).

Beginning at end of Neck Shaping, sew end of rows on Neck Ribbing together to halfway point; fold Collar to right side.

Design by Cathy Hardy.

beaded wedding set

Bethanne Hamlin brings along her knitting in A Turn in the Road. She's hurrying to make the fingerless gloves from this wedding set. Her son is getting married to a girl that Bethanne adores. The bride, who also knits, is sure to cherish these keepsakes from her happy day.

◼◼◼◻ **INTERMEDIATE**

Finished Sizes

Fingerless Gloves: 7¹⁄₂" circumference x 4³⁄₄" long (19 cm x 12 cm)
Veil: 9" (23 cm) diameter

MATERIALS

Super Fine Weight Yarn **SUPER FINE ① 1**
[2 ounces, 400 yards
(55 grams, 366 meters) per skein]:
  2 skeins
Straight knitting needles, size 2 (2.75 mm)
  or size needed for gauge
Set of 5 double pointed knitting needles,
  size 2 (2.75 mm) **or** size needed for gauge
Veil:
  #08 Seed Beads (silver lined crystal): 475
  Tulle - 40" x 55" (101.5 cm x 139.5 cm)
  ³⁄₈" (10 mm) wide Ribbon - 1¹⁄₄ yards
    (1.143 meters) or desired length
Fingerless Golves:
  #08 Seed Beads (silver lined crystal): 630
  #06 Seed Beads (silver lined crystal) - 14
  Accent crystals - 2
  Heart crystals - 2
  Split-ring markers - 3
  Stitch holder
Tapestry needle
Large eye beading needle

GAUGE: In Stockinette Stitch,
    16 sts and 23 rows/rnds = 2" (5 cm)

Techniques used:
• YO *(Fig. 5a, page 194)*
• M1 *(Figs. 10a & b, page 196)*
• K2 tog *(Fig. 11, page 196)*
• P2 tog *(Fig. 18, page 198)*
• adding new sts *(Figs. 6a & b, page 195)*

When instructed to slip a stitch, always slip as if to **purl** with yarn held to **right** side. This allows the bead to be positioned on the right side of the piece, in front of the slipped stitch.

WEDDING VEIL

Thread a large eye beading needle with the yarn and string 475 #08 seed beads, adding extra beads just to make sure you have enough.

RUFFLE

Using straight needles, cast on 215 sts.

Row 1: K1, ★ WYB slip 1, slide bead up (next to needle), K1; repeat from ★ across.

Row 2 (Right side): (K1, P4) across.

Instructions continued on page 158.

Row 7: (K2 tog, P1) across: 86 sts.

Row 8: K2, ★ WYF slip 1, slide bead up, K1; repeat from ★ across.

Row 9: Purl across.

Row 10 (Eyelet row): K1, (YO twice, K2 tog) across to last st, K1: 128 sts.

Row 11: P2, ★ purl into first YO letting second loop fall off needle, P1; repeat from ★ across: 86 sts.

BODY

Row 1: Knit across.

Row 2: P2, ★ WYB slip 1, slide bead up, P1; repeat from ★ across.

Row 3: Knit across.

Row 4: Purl across.

Row 5: K2, ★ WYF slip 1, slide bead up, K5; repeat from ★ across.

Row 6: Purl across.

Row 7: Knit across.

Row 8: Purl across.

Row 9: K5, ★ WYF slip 1, slide bead up; repeat from ★ across to last 2 sts, K2.

Rows 10-12: Repeat Rows 6-8.

Rows 13-21: Repeat Rows 5-12 once, then repeat Row 5 once **more**.

Row 3: (K4, P1) across.

Row 4: ★ K1, P2, slide bead up, P2; repeat from ★ across.

Row 5: (K4, P1) across.

Row 6: (K1, P2 tog twice) across: 129 sts.

CROWN

Row 1: (P1, P2 tog) 3 times, purl across to last 9 sts, (P2 tog, P1) 3 times: 80 sts.

Row 2: (K8, K2 tog) across: 72 sts.

Row 3 AND ALL WRONG SIDE ROWS: ★ P1, WYB slip 1, slide bead up; repeat from ★ across to last 2 sts, P2.

Row 4: (K7, K2 tog) across: 64 sts.

Row 6: (K6, K2 tog) across: 56 sts.

Row 8: (K5, K2 tog) across: 48 sts.

Row 10: (K4, K2 tog) across: 40 sts.

Row 12: (K3, K2 tog) across: 32 sts.

Row 14: (K2, K2 tog) across: 24 sts.

Row 16: (K1, K2 tog) across: 16 sts.

Row 18: K2 tog across: 8 sts.

Row 19: Repeat Row 3.

Cut yarn leaving a long end for sewing.

FINISHING

Thread tapestry needle with end and slip remaining sts onto needle; gather to close (not tightly) and secure end; sew side seam.

VEIL

Cut an oval from the tulle, approximately 40" x 55" (101.5 cm x 139.5 cm).

Using the diagram as a guide, sew a gathering stitch across the width, 5" (12.5 cm) from the top edge and gather to equal 3" (7.5 cm). Fold tulle along gathers and sew gathered edge to wrong side of knit cap centered at seam.

Beginning at seam, weave ribbon through Eyelet row; tie in a bow.

DIAGRAM

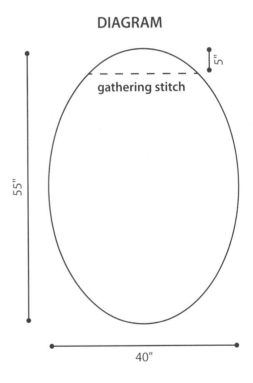

gathering stitch

5"

55"

40"

Instructions continued on page 160.

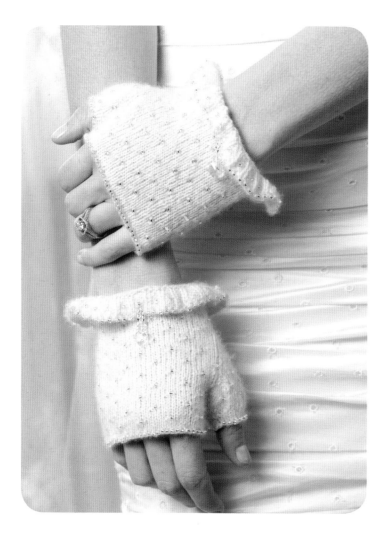

Row 4: ★ K1, P2, slide bead up, P2; repeat from ★ across.

Row 5: (K4, P1) across.

Row 6: (K1, P2 tog twice) across: 84 sts.

Row 7: (K2 tog, P1) across: 56 sts.

HAND

Slip 14 sts onto each of 4 double pointed needles *(Fig. 2c, page 193)*; place marker around first stitch to indicate beginning of rnd *(see Markers, page 191)*.

Rnd 1: With **wrong** side of Ruffle facing (right side of glove), (M1, knit across needle) 4 times: 60 sts.

Rnd 2: ★ K5, WYF slip 1, slide bead up; repeat from ★ around.

Rnds 3-5: Knit around.

Rnd 6: K2, WYF slip 1, slide bead up, ★ K5, WYF slip 1, slide bead up; repeat from ★ around to last 3 sts, K3.

Rnds 7-9: Knit around.

Rnds 10-18: Repeat Rnds 2-9 once, then repeat Rnd 2 once **more**.

GUSSET

Rnd 1 (Increase rnd): K 21, place marker, K1, M1, K3, M1, K1, place marker, knit across: 62 sts.

Rnd 2: Knit across to marker, P1, knit across to within one st of next marker, P1, knit across.

Rnd 3 (Increase rnd): Knit across to marker, P1, M1, knit across to within one st of next marker, M1, P1, knit across: 64 sts.

FINGERLESS GLOVES

Thread a large eye beading needle with the yarn and string 315 #08 seed beads, adding extra beads just to make sure you have enough.

RUFFLE

Using straight needles, cast on 140 sts.

Row 1: ★ K1, WYB slip 1, slide bead up (next to needle); repeat from ★ across to last 2 sts, K2.

Row 2 (Right side): (K1, P4) across.

Row 3: (K4, P1) across.

Rnd 4: K2, WYF slip 1, slide bead up, (K5, WYF slip 1, slide bead up) 3 times, P1, knit across to within one st of next marker, P1, WYF slip 1, slide bead up, (K5, WYF slip 1, slide bead up) 5 times, K3.

Rnds 5-7: Repeat Rnd 3, then repeat Rnds 2 and 3 once: 68 sts.

Rnd 8: (K5, WYF slip 1, slide bead up) 3 times, K3, P1, K5, WYF slip 1, slide bead up, K5, P1, K3, WYF slip 1, slide bead up, (K5, WYF slip 1, slide bead up) 5 times.

Rnds 9-19: Maintaining beading pattern, continue to increase 2 sts every other round in same manner, 6 times: 80 sts.

Rnd 20: Knit across in bead pattern to marker, remove marker, K1, slip next 23 sts onto st holder; **turn**, add on 3 sts, **turn**, knit across in bead pattern removing marker: 60 sts.

Work even in beading pattern for 11 rnds or to desired length.

Beaded Bind Off: With **wrong** side facing, K1, ★ slide bead up, K1, pass first stitch on right needle over second st; repeat from ★ until one st remains on right needle; cut yarn and pull end through st.

THUMB

With **right** side facing, slip sts from st holder onto 2 double pointed needles; pick up 13 sts across Hand **(Fig. 22b, page 199)**; place marker around first st to indicate beginning of round: 36 sts.

Rnds 1-5: Knit around maintaining bead pattern.

Rnd 6: K2 tog, (K2, K2 tog) around to last st, K1: 26 sts.

Rnd 7: Knit around.

Rnd 8: K2, (K2 tog, K2) around: 20 sts.

Rnds 9-11: Knit around maintaining bead pattern.

Turn and work Beaded Bind Off.

FINISHING
Sew side seam on Ruffle.

BEADED DECORATION
Using the diagram as a guide, string the beads in the following order: 4 #06 seed beads, accent bead, heart bead; then go back through the accent bead. String 3 more #06 seed beads, then go back through the first bead.

DIAGRAM

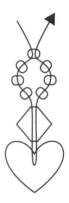

Using photo as a guide for placement, fold Ruffle toward Hand and sew beaded decoration in place, sewing through both layers. Be sure to have a right and a left glove.

Designs by Sandy Payne.

positively pretty pullover

Anne Marie Roche selected a rich red yarn for the sweater she wants to knit for herself. In Twenty Wishes, *Anne Marie has been in need of something to lift her spirits. A vivacious pullover with a pretty eyelet border will be a pleasant thing to look forward to!*

◼◼◼◻ **INTERMEDIATE**

Size	Finished Chest Measurement	
X-Small	32¹/₂"	(82.5 cm)
Small	35¹/₂"	(90 cm)
Medium	39"	(99 cm)
Large	45"	(114.5 cm)
X-Large	48¹/₂"	(123 cm)

Size Note: Instructions are written for sizes X-Small and Small in the first set of braces { }, with sizes Medium, Large and X-Large in the second set of braces. Instructions will be easier to read if you circle all the numbers pertaining to your size. If only one number is given, it applies to all sizes.

MATERIALS
Medium Weight Yarn ◖ 4 ◗
[2.8 ounces, 145 yards
(80 grams, 133 meters) per skein]:
  {7-8}{9-10-11} skeins
Straight knitting needles, size 7 (4.5 mm)
  or size needed for gauge
16" (40.5 cm) Circular knitting needle,
  size 5 (3.75 mm)
Stitch holders - 2
Yarn needle

GAUGE: With larger size needles,
in Stockinette Stitch,
20 sts and 26 rows = 4" (10 cm)

Techniques used:
• YO (*Fig. 5a, page 194*)
• knit increase (*Figs. 7a & b, page 195*)
• K2 tog (*Fig. 11, page 196*)
• slip 1, K1, PSSO (*Figs. 14a & b, page 197*)
• slip 1, K2 tog, PSSO (*Fig. 16, page 197*)
• slip 2 tog, K1, P2SSO (*Fig. 17, page 197*)
• P2 tog (*Fig. 18, page 198*)
• P2 tog tbl (*Fig. 19, page 198*)

BACK
BORDER
With straight needles, cast on
{83-91}{99-115-123} sts.

Row 1: P1, (K1, P1) across.

Row 2: K1, (P1, K1) across.

Row 3: P1, (K1, P1) across.

Row 4 (Right side): K3, K2 tog, YO, K1, YO, slip 1 as if to **knit**, K1, PSSO, K3, ★ K2 tog, YO, K1, YO, slip 1 as if to **knit**, K1, PSSO, K3; repeat from ★ across.

Instructions continued on page 164.

Row 5 AND ALL WRONG SIDE ROWS: Purl across.

Row 6: K2, K2 tog, YO, K3, YO, slip 1 as if to **knit**, K1, PSSO, ★ K1, K2 tog, YO, K3, YO, slip 1 as if to **knit**, K1, PSSO; repeat from ★ across to last 2 sts, K2.

Row 8: K1, K2 tog, YO, K5, ★ YO, slip 1 as if to **knit**, K2 tog, PSSO, YO, K5; repeat from ★ across to last 3 sts, YO, slip 1 as if to **knit**, K1, PSSO, K1.

Row 10: K1, slip 1 as if to **knit**, K1, PSSO, YO, K5, ★ YO, slip 2 tog as if to **knit**, K1, P2SSO, YO, K5; repeat from ★ across to last 3 sts, YO, K2 tog, K1.

Row 12: K1, slip 1 as if to **knit**, K1, PSSO, YO, K5, ★ YO, slip 2 tog as if to **knit**, K1, P2SSO, YO, K5; repeat from ★ across to last 3 sts, YO, K2 tog, K1.

Row 14: K3, ★ YO, slip 1 as if to **knit**, K1, PSSO, K1, K2 tog, YO, K3; repeat from ★ across.

Row 16: K4, YO, slip 1 as if to **knit**, K2 tog, PSSO, YO, ★ K5, YO, slip 1 as if to **knit**, K2 tog, PSSO, YO; repeat from ★ across to last 4 sts, K4.

BODY

Beginning with a purl row, work in Stockinette Stitch (purl one row, knit one row) until piece measures approximately {15-15}{15-16-16}"/{38-38}{38-40.5-40.5} cm from cast on edge, ending by working a **purl** row.

ARMHOLE SHAPING

Rows 1 and 2: Bind off {5-6}{6-8-10} sts, work across: {73-79}{87-99-103} sts.

Row 3 (Decrease row): Slip 1 as if to **knit**, K1, PSSO, knit across to last 2 sts, K2 tog: {71-77}{85-97-101} sts.

Row 4: Purl across.

Repeat Rows 3 and 4, {2-4}{4-6-7} times: {67-69}{77-85-87} sts.

Work even until Armholes measure approximately {7-8½}{9½-10-10½}"/{18-21.5}{24-25.5-26.5} cm, ending by working a **purl** row.

SHOULDER SHAPING

Rows 1-4: Bind off {6-6}{7-8-8} sts, work across: {43-45}{49-53-55} sts.

Rows 5 and 6: Bind off {6-6}{7-8-9} sts, work across: {31-33}{35-37-37} sts.

Slip remaining sts onto st holder; cut yarn.

FRONT

Work same as Back until Armholes measure approximately {3¹/₂-4³/₄}{5¹/₂-6-6¹/₄}"/{9-12}{14-15-16} cm, ending by working a **knit** row: {67-69}{77-85-87} sts.

NECK SHAPING

Both sides of the Neck are worked at the same time, using separate yarn for **each** side.

Row 1: Purl {24-24}{27-30-31} sts, slip next {19-21}{23-25-25} sts onto st holder; with second yarn, purl across: {24-24}{27-30-31} sts **each** side.

Row 2 (Decrease row): Knit across to within 2 sts of neck edge, K2 tog; with second yarn, slip 1 as if to **knit**, K1, PSSO, knit across: {23-23}{26-29-30} sts **each** side.

Row 3 (Decrease row): Purl across to within 2 sts of neck edge, P2 tog tbl; with second yarn, P2 tog, purl across: {22-22}{25-28-29} sts **each** side.

Row 4 (Decrease row): Knit across to within 2 sts of neck edge, K2 tog; with second yarn, slip 1 as if to **knit**, K1, PSSO, knit across: {21-21}{24-27-28} sts **each** side.

Row 5: Purl across; with second yarn, purl across.

Rows 6-11: Repeat Rows 4 and 5, 3 times: {18-18}{21-24-25} sts **each** side.

Work even until Front measures same as Back to Shoulder Shaping, ending by working a **purl** row.

SHOULDER SHAPING

Rows 1-4: Bind off {6-6}{7-8-8} sts, work across; with second yarn, work across: {6-6}{7-8-9} sts **each** side.

Row 5: Bind off remaining sts on first side; with second yarn, work across.

Bind off remaining sts.

SLEEVE (Make 2)
BORDER

With straight needles, cast on {43-43}{43-51-51} sts.

Row 1: P1, (K1, P1) across.

Row 2: K1, (P1, K1) across.

Row 3: P1, (K1, P1) across.

Row 4 (Right side): K3, ★ K2 tog, YO, K1, YO, slip 1 as if to **knit**, K1, PSSO, K3; repeat from ★ across.

Instructions continued on page 166.

SLEEVE

{12½-13½}{14½-15½-16¼}"

{15½-17½}{18-18-18¼}"

1¼"

{8½-8½}{8½-10¼-10¼}"

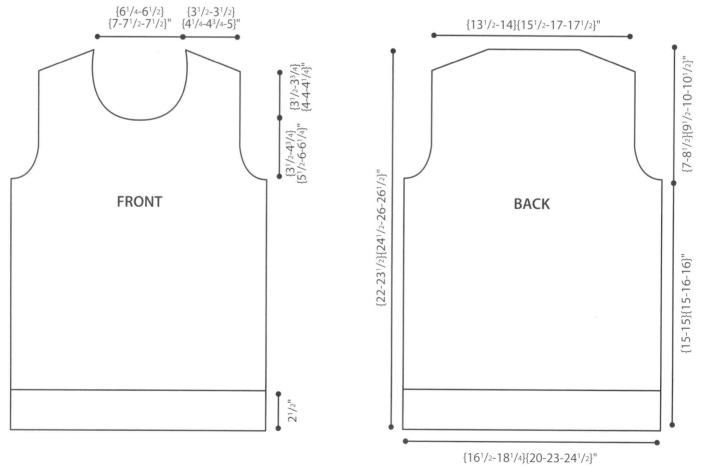

{6¼-6½}
{7-7½-7½}"

{3½-3½}
{4¼-4¾-5}"

{3½-3¾}
{4-4-4¼}"

{3½-4¾}
{5½-6-6¼}"

FRONT

2½"

{13½-14}{15½-17-17½}"

{7-8½}{9½-10-10½}"

{22-23½}{24½-26-26½}"

BACK

{15-15}{15-16-16}"

{16½-18¼}{20-23-24½}"

Note: Pullover includes two edge stitches.

Row 5: Purl across.

Row 6: K2, K2 tog, YO, K3, YO, slip 1 as if to **knit**, K1, PSSO, ★ K1, K2 tog, YO, K3, YO, slip 1 as if to **knit**, K1, PSSO; repeat from ★ across to last 2 sts, K2.

Row 7: Purl across.

Row 8: K1, K2 tog, YO, K5, ★ YO, slip 1 as if to **knit**, K2 tog, PSSO, YO, K5; repeat from ★ across to last 3 sts, YO, slip 1 as if to **knit**, K1, PSSO, K1.

BODY

Beginning with a purl row, work in Stockinette Stitch, increasing one stitch at **each** edge, every sixth row, {4-5}{15-8-15} times; then increase every eighth row, {6-7}{0-5-0} times **more** *(see Zeros, page 191)*: {63-67}{73-77-81} sts.

Work even until Sleeve measures approximately {15¹/₂-17¹/₂}{18-18-18¹/₄}"/{39.5-44.5}{45.5-45.5-46.5} cm from cast on edge, ending by working a **purl** row.

SLEEVE CAP

Rows 1 and 2: Bind off {5-6}{6-8-10} sts, work across: {53-55}{61-61-61} sts.

Row 3 (Decrease row): Slip 1 as if to **knit**, K1, PSSO, knit across to last 2 sts, K2 tog: {51-53}{59-59-59} sts.

Continue to decrease one stitch at **each** edge, every other row, {6-4}{5-2-1} time(s); then decrease every fourth row, {2-5}{7-9-10} times **more**: {35-35}{35-37-37} sts.

Bind off 4 sts at the beginning of the next 6 rows, work across: {11-11}{11-13-13} sts.

Bind off remaining sts.

FINISHING

Sew shoulder seams.

NECK RIBBING

With **right** side facing and using circular needle, pick up and knit {26-28}{30-30-32} sts evenly spaced along left Front Neck edge *(Fig. 22a, page 199)*, knit {19-21}{23-25-25} sts from Front st holder, pick up and knit {26-28}{30-30-32} sts evenly spaced along right Front Neck edge, slip {31-33}{35-37-37} sts from Back st holder onto empty point and knit across; place marker to indicate beginning of round *(see Markers, page 191)*: {102-110}{118-122-126} sts.

Work in K1, P1 ribbing for 3 rounds.

Bind off all sts **loosely** in ribbing.

Sew Sleeves to pullover, placing center of Sleeve Cap at shoulder seam and matching bound off stitches.

Weave underarm and side in one continuous seam *(Fig. 23, page 199)*.

Design by Cathy Hardy.

cody's dinosaur sweater

In A Good Yarn, shop owner Lydia Hoffman has added lots of new yarn and patterns to her store. This design is the perfect pullover for a youngster who likes dinosaurs, and that includes a little boy named Cody. His father is Brad, the handsome delivery driver who keeps dropping in to visit Lydia. She thinks it would be fun to make this sweater for Cody…and maybe another sweater for Brad.

■■■□ **INTERMEDIATE**

Size	ChestFinished MeasurementMeasurement		Chest	
4	24"	(61 cm)	27"	(68.5 cm)
6	25¹/₂"	(65 cm)	29¹/₂"	(75 cm)
8	27"	(68.5 cm)	31"	(78.5 cm)

Size Note: Instructions are written for size 4, with sizes 6 and 8 in braces { }. Instructions will be easier to read if you circle all the numbers pertaining to your size. If only one number is given, it applies to all sizes.

MATERIALS

Medium Weight Yarn

[3¹/₂ ounces, 174 yards (100 grams, 159 meters) per skein]:

  Main Color (Blue) - 4{4-5} skeins
  Brown - 1 skein

Straight knitting needles, sizes 4 (3.5 mm)
   and 6 (4 mm) **or** sizes needed for gauge
16" (40.5 cm) Circular needle, size 4 (3.5 mm)
Bobbins
Stitch holders - 2
Marker
Black bead for eye
Yarn needle

GAUGE: With larger size needles, in Stockinette Stitch, 20 sts and 26 rows = 4" (10 cm)

Techniques used:
• increasing evenly (*page 195*)
• knit increase (*Figs. 7a & b, page 195*)
• K2 tog (*Fig. 11, page 196*)
• slip 1, K1, PSSO (*Figs. 14a & b, page 197*)
• P2 tog (*Fig. 18, page 198*)
• SSP (*Fig. 21, page 198*)

The larger size needles are used for the Front and Back ribbing. The ribbing is intended to only pull in slightly, helping the dinosaur to be visible and not distorted.

SLEEVE (Make 2)
RIBBING

With Main Color and smaller size needles, cast on 30{32-32} sts.

Work in K1, P1 ribbing for 2{2-2¹/₂}"/5{5-6.5} cm increasing 4 sts evenly spaced across last row: 34{36-36} sts.

BODY

Change to larger size needles.

Row 1 (Right side)**:** Knit across.

Row 2: Purl across.

Rows 3 and 4: Repeat Rows 1 and 2.

Instructions continued on page 170.

Row 5 (Increase row): K1, increase, knit across to last 2 sts, increase, K1: 36{38-38} sts.

Working in Stockinette Stitch, continue to increase one stitch at **each** edge in same manner, every fourth row, 3{0-5} times **more** *(see Zeros, page 191)*; then increase every sixth row, 5{8-5} times: 52{54-58} sts.

Work even until Sleeve measures approximately $10\frac{1}{2}${$11\frac{3}{4}$-12}"/26.5{30-30.5} cm from cast on edge **or desired length to underarm**, ending by working a **purl** row.

SLEEVE CAP
Rows 1 and 2: Bind off 2{4-4} sts, work across: 48{46-50} sts.

Row 3 (Decrease row): K1, slip 1 as if to **knit**, K1, PSSO, knit across to last 3 sts, K2 tog, K1: 46{44-48} sts.

Row 4: Purl across.

Repeat Rows 3 and 4, 7{9-10} times: 32{26-28} sts.

Bind off 4{3-3} sts at the beginning of the next 4 rows, work across: 16{14-16} sts.

Bind off 4{3-4} sts at the beginning of the next 2 rows, work across: 8 sts.

Bind off remaining sts.

Use bobbins to hold the small amount of yarn needed to work each color change and also to keep the different color yarns from tangling. You'll need to wind a bobbin for each color change, using as many bobbins as necessary to avoid carrying the yarn across the back.

When changing colors, always pick up the new color yarn from **beneath** the dropped yarn and keep the color which has just been worked to the left **(Fig. 3b, page 193)**. This will prevent holes in the finished piece. Take extra care to keep your tension even.

FRONT CHART

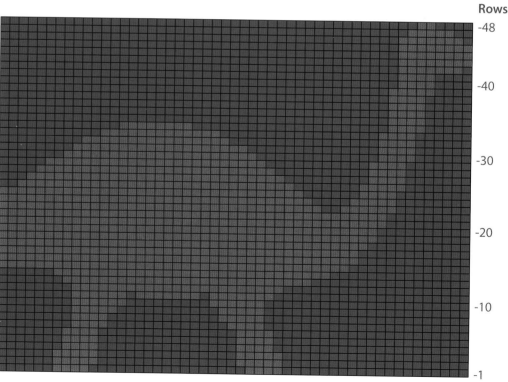

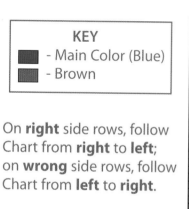

KEY
- Main Color (Blue)
- Brown

On **right** side rows, follow Chart from **right** to **left**; on **wrong** side rows, follow Chart from **left** to **right**.

Rows
-48
-40
-30
-20
-10
-1

FRONT
RIBBING

With Main Color and larger size needles, cast on 70{76-80} sts.

Work in K1, P1 ribbing for 1½{1½-2}"/4{4-5} cm.

BODY

Beginning with a **knit** row, work 4 rows in Stockinette Stitch.

Next Row: Knit across 19{25-29} sts, place marker to mark edge of Chart *(see Markers, page 191)*, knit across following Front Chart.

Continue to follow Chart.

Work even until Front measures approximately 10¼{11¼-12¼}"/26{28.5-31} cm from cast on edge, ending by working a **purl** row.

ARMHOLE SHAPING

Rows 1 and 2: Bind off 2{4-4} sts, work across: 66{68-72} sts.

Row 3 (Decrease row): K1, slip 1 as if to **knit**, K1, PSSO, knit across to last 3 sts, K2 tog, K1: 64{66-70} sts.

Row 4: Purl across.

Repeat Rows 3 and 4, 6{5-6} times: 52{56-58} sts.

Work even until Armholes measure approximately 3¼{3½-4}"/8.5{9-10} cm, ending by working a **knit** row.

NECK SHAPING

Both sides of Neck are worked at the same time, using separate yarn for **each** side.

Row 1: Purl 19{21-21} sts, slip next 14{14-16} sts onto st holder; with second yarn, purl across: 19{21-21} sts **each** side.

Row 2 (Decrease row): Knit across to within 2 sts of neck edge, K2 tog; with second yarn, slip 1 as if to **knit**, K1, PSSO, knit across: 18{20-20} sts **each** side.

Row 3 (Decrease row): Purl across to within 2 sts of neck edge, P2 tog; with second yarn, SSP, purl across: 17{19-19} sts **each** side.

Row 4 (Decrease row): Knit across to within 2 sts of neck edge, K2 tog; with second yarn, slip 1 as if to **knit**, K1, PSSO, knit across: 16{18-18} sts **each** side.

Row 5: Purl across; with second yarn, purl across.

Rows 6-9: Repeat Rows 4 and 5 twice: 14{16-16} sts **each** side.

Work even until Armholes measure approximately 5¼{5¾-6¼}"/13.5{14.5-16} cm, ending by working a **knit** row.

SHOULDER SHAPING

Rows 1 and 2: Bind off 4{5-5} sts, work across; with second yarn, work across: 10{11-11} sts **each** side.

Rows 3 and 4: Bind off 5 sts, work across; with second yarn, work across: 5{6-6} sts **each** side.

Row 5: Bind off remaining sts on first side; with second yarn, work across.

Bind off remaining sts.

Instructions continued on page 172.

BACK

RIBBING

With Main Color and larger size needles, cast on 70{76-80} sts.

Work in K1, P1 ribbing for 1¹/₂{1¹/₂-2}"/4{4-5} cm.

BODY

Beginning with a **knit** row, work 15 rows in Stockinette Stitch.

Next Row: Purl across 39{45-49} sts, place marker to mark edge of Chart, purl across following Back Chart.

Continue to follow Chart.

BACK CHART

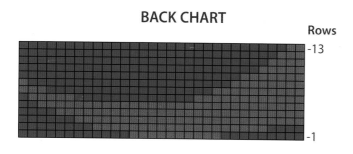

Rows
-13

-1

Work even until Back measures same as Front to Armholes, ending by working a **purl** row.

ARMHOLE SHAPING

Work Shaping same as Front, then work even until Armholes measure same as Front to Shoulder Shaping, ending by working a **knit** row: 52{56-58} sts.

SHOULDER SHAPING

Rows 1 and 2: Bind off 4{5-5} sts, work across: 44{46-48} sts.

Rows 3 and 4: Bind off 5 sts, work across: 34{36-38} sts.

Rows 5 and 6: Bind off 5{6-6} sts, work across: 24{24-26} sts.

Slip remaining sts onto st holder.

FINISHING

Sew bead to dinosaur for eye.

Sew shoulder seams.

NECK RIBBING

With **right** side facing, Main Color, and using circular needle, knit 24{24-26} sts from Back st holder, pick up 17{19-19} sts evenly spaced along Left Neck edge (*Figs. 22a & b, page 199*), knit 14{14-16} sts from Front st holder, pick up 17{19-19} sts evenly spaced along Right Neck edge, place marker to mark beginning of round: 72{76-80} sts.

Work in K1, P1 ribbing around for 1" (2.5 cm).

Bind off all sts **loosely** in ribbing.

Sew Sleeves to sweater, placing center of Sleeve Cap at shoulder seam and matching bound off stitches.

Weave underarm and side in one continuous seam (*Fig. 23, page 199*).

Weave in all yarn ends.

harvey's vest

Harvey isn't going to like the vest that his neighbor Macy Roth is knitting for him—at least, that's what he's sure to tell her! But in Hannah's List, *Macy knows her elderly neighbor deals with emotions by being cantankerous. Truth is, Harvey will enjoy the vest the same way he does Macy's casseroles—very much—as long as she isn't looking.*

Shown on page 175.

■■■□ INTERMEDIATE

Size	Finished Chest Measurement	
34	36½"	(92.5 cm)
36	38"	(96.5 cm)
38	40"	(101.5 cm)
40	42½"	(108 cm)
42	44"	(112 cm)
44	46"	(117 cm)

Size Note: Instructions are written with sizes 34, 36, and 38 in the first set of braces {} and sizes 40, 42, and 44 in the second set of braces. Instructions will be easier to read if you circle all the numbers pertaining to your size. If only one number is given, it applies to all sizes.

MATERIALS

Medium Weight Yarn
[3.5 ounces, 223 yards
(100 grams, 205 meters) per skein]:
   {4-4-4}{5-5-5} skeins
Straight knitting needles, size 8 (5 mm) **or**
   size needed for gauge
29" (73.5 cm) Circular knitting needle,
   size 8 (5 mm)
Markers
Yarn needle
¾" (19 mm) Buttons - 5
Sewing needle and thread

GAUGE: In pattern,
   19 sts and 28 rows = 4" (10 cm)

Gauge Swatch: 4" (10 cm) square
Cast on 19 sts.
Work same as Back for 28 rows.
Bind off all sts.

Techniques used:
- YO *(Fig. 5a, page 194)*
- K2 tog *(Fig. 11, page 196)*
- SSK *(Figs. 13a-c, page 196)*;
- P2 tog *(Fig. 18, page 198)*;
- SSP *(Fig. 21, page 198)*;

BACK

Cast on {89-93-97}{103-107-111} sts.

Rows 1-8: Knit across.

Row 9: P2, K1, (P1, K1) across to last 2 sts, P2.

Instructions continued on page 174.

RIGHT FRONT

Cast on {41-43-45}{49-51-53} sts.

Work same as Back, page 175, to Armhole Shaping.

ARMHOLE & NECK SHAPING

Maintain established pattern throughout.

Row 1: Bind off {7-7-8}{10-10-11} sts, knit across: {34-36-37}{39-41-42} sts.

Row 2: Knit across to last 3 sts, K2 tog, K1: {33-35-36}{38-40-41} sts.

Row 3: P1, P2 tog, work across: {32-34-35}{37-39-40} sts.

Row 4: K1, SSK, work across to last 3 sts, K2 tog, K1: {30-32-33}{35-37-38} sts.

Row 5: K1, K2 tog, knit across: {29-31-32}{34-36-37} sts.

Row 6: Knit across to last 3 sts, K2 tog, K1: {28-30-31}{33-35-36} sts.

Row 7: Work across.

Row 8 (Neck decrease row)**:** K1, SSK, work across: {27-29-30}{32-34-35} sts.

Continue to decrease one stitch at Neck edge, every fourth row, {5-7-12}{15-15-15} times **more**; then decrease every sixth row, {5-4-1}{0-0-0} time(s) *(see Zeros, page 191)*: {17-18-17}{17-19-20} sts.

Work even until Right Front measures same as Back to Shoulder Shaping, ending by working a **right** side row.

SHOULDER SHAPING

Row 1: Bind off {6-6-6}{6-6-7} sts, work across: {11-12-11}{11-13-13} sts.

Row 2: Work across.

Rows 3 and 4: Repeat Rows 1 and 2: {5-6-5}{5-7-6} sts.

Bind off remaining sts in pattern leaving a long end for sewing.

LEFT FRONT

Cast on {41-43-45}{49-51-53} sts.

Work same as Back to Armhole Shaping, ending by working Row 9.

ARMHOLE & NECK SHAPING

Maintain established pattern throughout.

Row 1: Bind off {7-7-8}{10-10-11} sts, work across: {34-36-37}{39-41-42} sts.

Row 2: Knit across.

Row 3: K1, SSK, knit across to last 3 sts, K2 tog, K1: {32-34-35}{37-39-40} sts.

Row 4: Work across to last 3 sts, SSP, P1: {31-33-34}{36-38-39} sts.

Row 5: K1, SSK, work across: {30-32-33}{35-37-38} sts.

Row 6: Knit across to last 3 sts, SSK, K1: {29-31-32} {34-36-37} sts.

Row 7: K1, SSK, knit across to last 3 sts, K2 tog, K1: {27-29-30}{32-34-35} sts.

Continue to decrease one stitch at Neck edge, every fourth row, {5-7-12}{15-15-15} times **more**; then decrease every sixth row, {5-4-1}{0-0-0} time(s): {17-18-17}{17-19-20} sts.

Work even until Left Front measures same as Back to Shoulder Shaping, ending by working a **wrong** side row.

SHOULDER SHAPING
Work same as Right Front.

FINISHING
Using long ends, sew shoulder seams.

FRONT BAND
With **right** side facing and using circular needle, pick up {64-66-66}{68-68-70} sts evenly spaced along Right Front edge to Neck Shaping *(Figs. 22a & b, page 199)*, pick up {46-48-50}{54-54-56} sts evenly spaced along Neck Shaping, pick up {31-33-37} {39-39-39} sts across Back Neck edge, pick up {46-48-50}{54-54-56} sts evenly spaced along Left Front Neck Shaping, pick up {64-66-66}{68-68-70} sts evenly spaced along Left Front edge: {251-261-269} {283-283-291} sts.

Rows 1-3: Knit across.

Place markers on Left Front for buttonholes, placing first marker approximately ³/₄" (19 mm) above cast on edge and last marker at beginning of Neck Shaping, then evenly spacing markers for remaining 3 buttonholes.

Row 4 (Buttonhole row): Knit across to first marker, K2 tog, YO, ★ knit across to next marker, K2 tog, YO; repeat from ★ 3 times **more**, knit across.

Rows 5-8: Knit across.

Bind off all sts in **knit**.

ARMHOLE BAND
With **right** side facing and using circular needle, pick up {96-98-102}{114-114-118} sts evenly spaced along Armhole edge.

Rows 1-8: Knit across.

Bind off all sts in **knit**.

Repeat on remaining Armhole.

Weave side seams *(Fig. 23, page 199)*.

Sew buttons to Right Front opposite buttonholes.

Design by Sarah J. Green.

Thank you for helping WARM UP AMERICA!

Since 1991, Warm Up America! volunteers have donated more than a quarter of a million handmade afghans to the homeless, victims of natural disaster, residents of battered women's shelters, and to many others who are in need. Whether the volunteers work alone or in groups with their friends, neighbors, or co-workers, they enjoy the community spirit of helping others.

In these pages, you'll find patterns for seventeen 7" x 9" blocks to knit, all gathered from the *Knit Along with Debbie Macomber* book series. These blocks are great portable projects and can be mixed or matched to make lovely and practical blankets. Debbie encourages all her friends to donate a little yarn and knitting time to help Warm Up America! If you are able to provide a new, completed afghan, please donate it to any charity or social service agency in your community.

Visit www.warmupamerica.com for more information about this exciting volunteer opportunity.

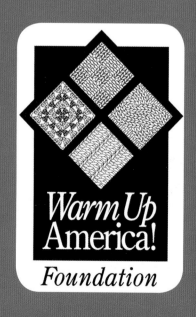

REMEMBER, JUST A LITTLE BIT OF YARN CAN MAKE A BIG DIFFERENCE TO SOMEONE IN NEED!

Basic patchwork afghans are made of forty-nine 7" x 9" (18 cm x 23 cm) rectangular blocks that are sewn together. Any pattern stitch can be used for the rectangle. Use acrylic medium weight yarn. For a knit block use size 8 (5 mm) straight knitting needles or size needed to obtain the gauge of 9 stitches to 2" (5 cm).

warm up america!

1. SEED STITCH BLOCK

Multiple of 2 sts.

Cast on 32 sts.

Row 1 (Right side): (K1, P1) across.

Row 2: (P1, K1) across.

Repeat Rows 1 and 2 for pattern until Block measures approximately 9" (23 cm) from cast on edge.

Bind off all sts in pattern.

2. CLUSTER RIB BLOCK

Multiple of 3 sts + 1.

Technique used:
• YO *(Fig. 5a, page 194)*

Cast on 34 sts.

Row 1 (Right side): P1, (K2, P1) across.

Row 2: K1, ★ YO, K2, with left needle bring the YO over the 2 knit sts and off the right needle, K1; repeat from ★ across.

Repeat Rows 1 and 2 for pattern until Block measures approximately 9" (23 cm) from cast on edge, ending by working Row 2.

Bind off all sts in pattern.

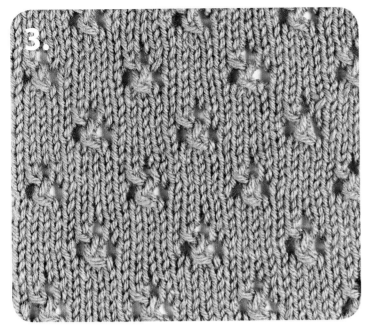

3. CLOVERLEAF EYELET BLOCK

Multiple of 8 sts + 7.

Techniques used:
- YO *(Fig. 5a, page 194)*
- SSK *(Fig. 13, page 196)*
- slip 1, K2 tog, PSSO *(Fig. 16, page 197)*

Cast on 31 sts.

Row 1 AND ALL WRONG SIDE ROWS: Purl across.

Row 2: Knit across.

Row 4: K2, YO, slip 1 as if to **knit**, K2 tog, PSSO, ★ YO, K5, YO, slip 1 as if to **knit**, K2 tog, PSSO; repeat from ★ across to last 2 sts, YO, K2.

Row 6: K3, YO, SSK, (K6, YO, SSK) across to last 2 sts, K2.

Row 8: Knit across.

Row 10: K6, YO, slip 1 as if to **knit**, K2 tog, PSSO, ★ YO, K5, YO, slip 1 as if to **knit**, K2 tog, PSSO; repeat from ★ across to last 6 sts, YO, K6.

Row 12: K7, (YO, SSK, K6) across.

Repeat Rows 1-12 for pattern until Block measures approximately 9" (23 cm) from cast on edge, ending by working Row 3 or Row 9.

Bind off all sts in knit.

4. CHECKERBOARD BLOCK

Multiple of 6 sts.

Cast on 30 sts.

Rows 1-3: (P3, K3) across.

Rows 4-6: (K3, P3) across.

Repeat Rows 1-6 for pattern until Block measures approximately 9" (23 cm) from cast on edge, ending by working Row 3 or Row 6.

Bind off all sts in pattern.

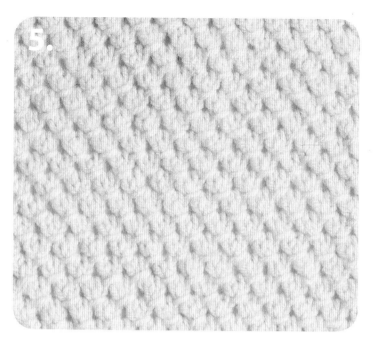

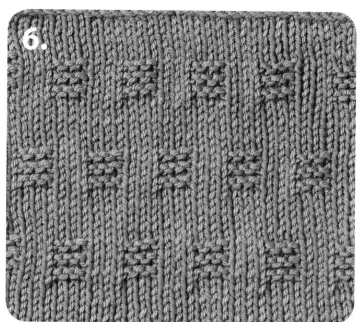

5. CROCUS BUDS BLOCK

Multiple of 2 sts + 1.

Technique used:
• YO (*Fig. 5a, page 194*)

Cast on 31 sts.

Row 1 (Right side): K1, (YO, K2) across.

Row 2: P4, with left needle bring the third st on right needle over the first 2 sts and off the needle, ★ P3, with left needle bring the third st on right needle over the first 2 sts and off the needle; repeat from ★ across.

Row 3: (K2, YO) across to last st, K1.

Row 4: ★ P3, with left needle bring the third st on right needle over the first 2 sts and off the needle; repeat from ★ across to last st, P1.

Repeat Rows 1-4 for pattern until Block measures approximately 9" (23 cm) from cast on edge, ending by working Row 2 or Row 4.

Bind off all sts in knit.

6. CHECKS BLOCK

Multiple of 6 sts + 3.

Cast on 33 sts.

Row 1: Purl across.

Row 2 (Right side): Knit across.

Rows 3-6: Repeat Rows 1 and 2 twice.

Row 7: Purl across.

Row 8: K3, (P3, K3) across.

Rows 9-12: Repeat Rows 7 and 8 twice.

Rows 13-18: Repeat Rows 1 and 2, 3 times.

Row 19: Purl across.

Row 20: P3, (K3, P3) across.

Rows 21-24: Repeat Rows 19 and 20 twice.

Repeat Rows 1-24 for pattern until Block measures approximately 9" (23 cm) from cast on edge, ending by working Row 6 or Row 18. Bind off all sts in purl.

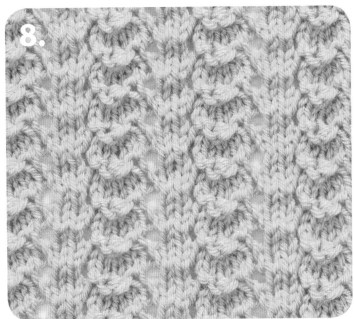

7. LITTLE FOUNTAIN BLOCK

Multiple of 4 sts + 1.

Techniques used:
• YO (*Fig. 5a, page 194*)
• slip 1, K2 tog, PSSO (*Fig. 16, page 197*)

Cast on 33 sts.

Row 1 (Right side): K1, (YO, K3, YO, K1) across.

Row 2: Purl across.

Row 3: K2, slip 1 as if to **knit**, K2 tog, PSSO, ★ K3, slip 1 as if to **knit**, K2 tog, PSSO; repeat from ★ across to last 2 sts, K2.

Row 4: Purl across.

Repeat Rows 1-4 for pattern until Block measures approximately 9" (23 cm) from cast on edge, ending by working Row 4.

Bind off all sts in knit.

8. LITTLE SHELLS

Multiple of 7 sts + 2.

Techniques used:
• YO (*Figs. 5c & d, page 194*)
• P3 tog (*Fig. 20, page 198*)

Cast on 30 sts.

Row 1 (Right side): Knit across.

Row 2: Purl across.

Row 3: K2, ★ YO, P1, P3 tog, P1, YO, K2; repeat from ★ across.

Row 4: Purl across.

Repeat Rows 1-4 for pattern until Block measures approximately 9" (23 cm) from cast on edge, ending by working a **wrong** side row.

Bind off all sts in knit.

9. 2-COLOR WOVEN BLOCK

Multiple of 2 sts + 1.

You will need two colors.

Using Color A, cast on 31 sts.

When instructed to slip a stitch, always slip as if to **purl** with yarn held **loosely** to **right** side so that the carried strand shows on the right side forming the woven look.

Row 1 (Right side)**:** K1, (slip 1, K1) across.

Row 2: P2, slip 1, (P1, slip 1) across to last 2 sts, P2.

Repeat Rows 1 and 2 changing colors every 2 rows, and carrying unused yarn loosely along side of piece, until Block measures approximately 9" (23 cm) from cast on edge, ending by working a **right** side row.

Bind off all sts in purl.

10. TWISTED SEED BLOCK

Multiple of 2 sts + 1.

Techniques used:
• K1 tbl (**Fig. 4, page 193**)

Cast on 31 sts.

Row 1: P1, (K1, P1) across.

Row 2 (Right side)**:** K1, (K1 tbl, K1) across.

Row 3: P2, K1, (P1, K1) across to last 2 sts, P2.

Row 4: K2, K1 tbl, (K1, K1 tbl) across to last 2 sts, K2.

Repeat Rows 1-4 for pattern until Block measures approximately 9" (23 cm) from cast on edge, ending by working a **wrong** side row.

Bind off all sts in pattern.

11.

11. SLIP STITCH BOXES BLOCK

Multiple of 7 sts + 1.

Additional materials: Cable needle

When instructed to slip a stitch, always slip as if to **purl.**

Cast on 36 sts.

Row 1 (Right side)**:** Knit across.

Row 2: P3, K2, (P5, K2) across to last 3 sts, P3.

Row 3: Knit across.

Rows 4 and 5: Repeat Rows 2 and 3.

Row 6: (K2, WYF slip 1) twice, (K3, WYF slip 1, K2, WYF slip 1) across to last 2 sts, K2.

Row 7: P2, WYB slip 1, K2, WYB slip 1, (P3, WYB slip 1, K2, WYB slip 1) across to last 2 sts, P2.

Row 8: (K2, WYF slip 1) twice, (K3, WYF slip 1, K2, WYF slip 1) across to last 2 sts, K2.

Row 9: K2, slip next st onto cable needle and hold in **front** of work, knit third st on left needle making sure not to drop off, then knit first and second sts letting all 3 sts drop off left needle, K1 from cable needle, ★ K3, slip next st onto cable needle and hold in **front** of work, knit third st on left needle making sure not to drop off, then knit first and second sts letting all 3 sts drop off left needle, K1 from cable needle; repeat from ★ across to last 2 sts, K2.

Row 10: P3, K2, (P5, K2) across to last 3 sts, P3.

Repeat Rows 1-10 for pattern until Block measures approximately 9" (23 cm) from cast on edge, ending by working a **wrong** side row.

Bind off all sts in pattern.

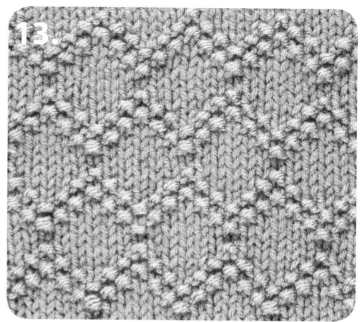

12. CABLE & BOBBLES BLOCK

Additional materials: cable needle

Cast on 33 sts.

Row 1 (Right side)**:** P 14, slip next 3 sts onto cable needle and hold in **back** of work, K2 from left needle, K3 from cable needle, purl across.

Row 2: K 14, P5, K 14.

Row 3: P 14, K5, P 14.

Row 4: K 14, P5, K 14.

Row 5: P 14, K2, (K, P, K, P, K) all in next st, pass second, third, fourth, and fifth sts on right needle over first st, K2, P 14.

Row 6: K 14, P5, K 14.

Row 7: P 14, K5, P 14.

Row 8: K 14, P5, K 14.

Repeat Rows 1-8 for pattern until Block measures approximately 9" (23 cm) from cast on edge, ending by working Row 1. Bind off all sts in pattern.

13. SEED STITCH ZIGZAG BLOCK

Multiple of 6 sts + 1.

Cast on 31 sts.

Row 1 (Right side)**:** Knit across.

Row 2: Purl across.

Row 3: P1, (K5, P1) across.

Row 4: P1, ★ K1, P3, K1, P1; repeat from ★ across.

Rows 5 and 6: P1, (K1, P1) across.

Row 7: K2, P1, K1, P1, ★ K3, P1, K1, P1; repeat from ★ across to last 2 sts, K2.

Row 8: P3, K1, (P5, K1) across to last 3 sts, P3.

Row 9: Knit across.

Row 10: Purl across.

Row 11: K3, P1, (K5, P1) across to last 3 sts, K3.

Row 12: P2, K1, P1, K1, ★ P3, K1, P1, K1; repeat from ★ across to last 2 sts, P2.

Rows 13 and 14: K1, (P1, K1) across.

Row 15: K1, ★ P1, K3, P1, K1; repeat from ★ across.

Row 16: K1, (P5, K1) across.

Repeat Rows 1-16 until Block measures approximately 9" (23 cm) from cast on edge, ending by working a **right** side row.

Bind off all sts in knit.

14. MOSS ZIGZAG BLOCK

Multiple of 7 sts.

Cast on 28 sts.

Row 1 (Right side): (P1, K1, P1, K4) across.

Row 2: (P4, K1, P1, K1) across.

Row 3: (K1, P1) twice, (K4, P1, K1, P1) across to last 3 sts, K3.

Row 4: P3, K1, P1, K1, (P4, K1, P1, K1) across to last st, P1.

Row 5: K2, P1, K1, P1, (K4, P1, K1, P1) across to last 2 sts, K2.

Row 6: P2, K1, P1, K1, (P4, K1, P1, K1) across to last 2 sts, P2.

Row 7: K3, P1, K1, P1, (K4, P1, K1, P1) across to last st, K1.

Row 8: (P1, K1) twice, (P4, K1, P1, K1) across to last 3 sts, P3.

Row 9: (K4, P1, K1, P1) across.

Row 10: (K1, P1, K1, P4) across.

Rows 11 and 12: Repeat Rows 7 and 8.

Rows 13 and 14: Repeat Rows 5 and 6.

Rows 15 and 16: Repeat Rows 3 and 4.

Repeat Rows 1-16 for pattern until Block measures approximately 9" (23 cm) from cast on edge.

Bind off all sts in pattern.

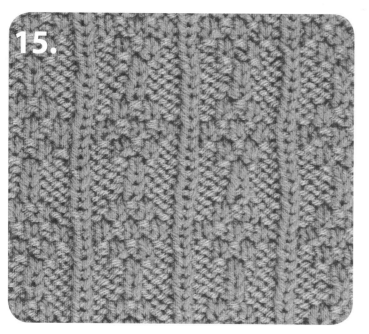

15. MOSS PANELS BLOCK

Multiple of 8 + 7 sts.

Cast on 31 sts.

Row 1 (Right side): Purl across.

Row 2: K3, (P1, K3) across.

Row 3: P3, (K1, P3) across.

Row 4: K2, P1, K1, P1, K2, ★ P1, K2, P1, K1, P1, K2; repeat from ★ 2 times **more.**

Row 5: P2, K1, P1, K1, P2, ★ K1, P2, K1, P1, K1, P2; repeat from ★ 2 times **more.**

Row 6: K1, (P1, K1) across.

Row 7: P1, (K1, P1) across.

Rows 8 and 9: Repeat Rows 4 and 5.

Rows 10 and 11: Repeat Rows 2 and 3.

Repeat Rows 2-11 until Block measures approximately 9" (23 cm) from cast on edge, ending by working a **right** side row. Bind off all sts.

16. KNIT QUILTED LACE BLOCK

Multiple of 6 sts + 1.

When instructed to slip stitches, always slip as if to **purl**, with yarn held **loosely** to **right** side so that the carried strand shows on the right side.

Cast on 31 sts.

Row 1 AND ALL WRONG SIDE ROWS: Purl across.

Row 2: K4, slip 5, (K1, slip 5) 3 times, K4.

Row 4: K6, K1 under strand (*Fig. A*), (K5, K1 under strand) 3 times, K6.

Fig. A

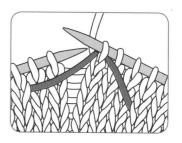

Row 6: K3, slip 3, K1, (slip 5, K1) 3 times, slip 3, K3.

Row 8: K3, K1 under strand, (K5, K1 under strand) 4 times, K3.

Repeat Rows 1-8 for pattern until Block measures approximately 9" (23 cm) from cast on edge, ending by working Row 1 or Row 5.

Bind off all sts in knit.

17. DIAMONDS BLOCK
Multiple of 10 sts + 1.

Cast on 31 sts.

Row 1 (Right side): K5, P1, K3, P1, K1, P1, ★ (K3, P1) twice, K1, P1; repeat from ★ across to last 9 sts, K3, P1, K5.

Row 2: P5, K1, P3, K1, P1, K1, ★ (P3, K1) twice, P1, K1; repeat from ★ across to last 9 sts, P3, K1, P5.

Row 3: K4, P1, K1, P1, ★ (K3, P1) twice, K1, P1; repeat from ★ across to last 4 sts, K4.

Row 4: P4, K1, P1, K1, ★ (P3, K1) twice, P1, K1; repeat from ★ across to last 4 sts, P4.

Row 5: K3, P1, (K1, P1) twice, ★ (K2, P1) twice, (K1, P1) twice; repeat from ★ across to last 3 sts, K3.

Row 6: P3, K1, (P1, K1) twice, ★ (P2, K1) twice, (P1, K1) twice; repeat from ★ across to last 3 sts, P3.

Row 7: K4, P1, K1, P1, ★ (K3, P1) twice, K1, P1; repeat from ★ across to last 4 sts, K4.

Row 8: P4, K1, P1, K1, ★ (P3, K1) twice, P1, K1; repeat from ★ across to last 4 sts, P4.

Row 9: K5, P1, K3, P1, K1, P1, ★ (K3, P1) twice, K1, P1; repeat from ★ across to last 9 sts, K3, P1, K5.

Row 10: P5, K1, P3, K1, P1, K1, ★ (P3, K1) twice, P1, K1; repeat from ★ across to last 9 sts, P3, K1, P5.

Row 11: K5, P1, K2, P1, (K1, P1) twice, ★ (K2, P1) twice, (K1, P1) twice; repeat from ★ across to last 8 sts, K2, P1, K5.

Row 12: P5, K1, P2, K1, (P1, K1) twice, ★ (P2, K1) twice, (P1, K1) twice; repeat from ★ across to last 8 sts, P2, K1, P5.

Repeat Rows 1-12 for pattern until Block measures approximately 9" (23 cm) from cast on edge, ending by working a **wrong** side row.

Bind off all sts in knit.

ASSEMBLY
Whipstitch Blocks together *(Fig. 24, page 199)*, forming 7 vertical strips of 7 Blocks each and measuring 7" x 63" (18 cm x 160 cm); whipstitch strips together in same manner.

Weave in all yarn ends.

general instructions

ABBREVIATIONS

C2B	cable 2 back
C4B	cable 4 back
C6B	cable 6 back
C2F	cable 2 front
C4F	cable 4 front
C6F	cable 6 front
cm	centimeters
K	knit
M1	make one
mm	millimeters
P	purl
P2SSO	pass 2 slipped stitches over
PSSO	pass slipped stitch over
Rnd(s)	round(s)
SSK	slip, slip, knit
SSP	slip, slip, purl
st(s)	stitch(es)
tbl	through back loop
tog	together
WYB	with yarn in back
WYF	with yarn in front
YO	yarn over

★ — work instructions following ★ as many **more** times as indicated in addition to the first time.

† to † — work all instructions from first † to second † **as many** times as specified.

( ) or [ ] — work enclosed instructions **as many** times as specified by the number immediately following **or** work all enclosed instructions in the stitch indicated **or** contains explanatory remarks.

colon (:) — the number given after a colon at the end of a row or round denotes the number of stitches you should have on that row or round.

work even — work without increasing or decreasing in the established pattern.

KNITTING NEEDLES		
UNITED STATES	ENGLISH U.K.	METRIC (mm)
0	13	2
1	12	2.25
2	11	2.75
3	10	3.25
4	9	3.5
5	8	3.75
6	7	4
7	6	4.5
8	5	5
9	4	5.5
10	3	6
10½	2	6.5
11	1	8
13	00	9
15	000	10
17	---	12.75

Yarn Weight Symbol & Names	LACE 0	SUPER FINE 1	FINE 2	LIGHT 3	MEDIUM 4	BULKY 5	SUPER BULKY 6
Type of Yarns in Category	Fingering, size 10 crochet thread	Sock, Fingering, Baby	Sport, Baby	DK, Light Worsted	Worsted, Afghan, Aran	Chunky, Craft, Rug	Bulky, Roving
Knit Gauge Range* in Stockinette St to 4" (10 cm)	33-40** sts	27-32 sts	23-26 sts	21-24 sts	16-20 sts	12-15 sts	6-11 sts
Advised Needle Size Range	000-1	1 to 3	3 to 5	5 to 7	7 to 9	9 to 11	11 and larger

*GUIDELINES ONLY: The chart above reflects the most commonly used gauges and needle sizes for specific yarn categories.

** Lace weight yarns are usually knitted on larger needles to create lacy openwork patterns. Accordingly, a gauge range is difficult to determine. Always follow the gauge stated in your pattern.

GAUGE

Exact gauge is **essential** for proper size. Before beginning your project, make a sample swatch in the yarn and needle specified in the individual instructions. After completing the swatch, measure it, counting your stitches and rows or rounds carefully. If your swatch is larger or smaller than specified, **make another, changing needle size to get the correct gauge**. Keep trying until you find the size needles that will give you the specified gauge. Once proper gauge is obtained, measure width approximately every 3" (7.5 cm) to be sure gauge remains consistent.

MARKERS

As a convenience to you, we have used markers to mark the beginning of a round, or to mark the placement of a pattern or increases and decreases. Place markers as instructed. You may use purchased markers or tie a length of contrasting color yarn around the needle. When you reach a marker, slip it from the left needle to the right needle; remove it when no longer needed. When using double pointed needles, a split-ring marker can be placed around the first stitch in the round to indicate the beginning of the round. Move it up at the end of each round.

ZEROS

To consolidate the length of an involved pattern, zeros are sometimes used so that all sizes can be combined. For example, knit 0{2-0-2} means that the first and third sizes would do nothing, and the second and fourth sizes would knit 2 sts.

FOLLOWING LACE CHARTS

Lace designs can be knit from a chart. You might find this easier than following written instructions, as you can see what the pattern looks like and you can also see each row at a glance. If you've never followed a chart before, you can refer to the chart while you read the instructions until you are comfortable following a chart.

The chart shows each stitch as a square. Refer to the key given with each chart for a symbol guide of the stitches used. Visualize the chart as your fabric, beginning at the bottom edge and looking at the right side.

When working in rounds, always follow the chart from right to left. For ease in following the chart, place a ruler on the chart above the row being worked to help keep your place.

KNIT TERMINOLOGY	
UNITED STATES	**INTERNATIONAL**
gauge =	tension
bind off =	cast off
yarn over (YO) =	yarn forward (yfwd) **or**
	yarn around needle (yrn)

◼◻◻◻ BEGINNER	Projects for first-time knitters using basic knit and purl stitches. Minimal shaping.
◼◼◻◻ EASY	Projects using basic stitches, repetitive stitch patterns, simple color changes, and simple shaping and finishing.
◼◼◼◻ INTERMEDIATE	Projects with a variety of stitches, such as basic cables and lace, simple intarsia, double-pointed needles and knitting in the round needle techniques, mid-level shaping and finishing.
◼◼◼◼ EXPERIENCED	Projects using advanced techniques and stitches, such as short rows, fair isle, more intricate intarsia, cables, lace patterns, and numerous color changes.

CIRCULAR NEEDLES

Since you need to use a shorter length needle then the measurement of stitches on your needle, it is sometimes necessary to use a circular needle.

USING ONE CIRCULAR NEEDLE

Using a circular needle, cast on as many stitches as instructed. Untwist and straighten the stitches on the needle to be sure that the cast on ridge lays on the inside of the needle and never rolls around the needle.

Hold the needle so that the ball of yarn is attached to the stitch closest to the **right** hand point. Working each round on the outside of the circle, with the **right** side of the knitting facing you, work across the stitches on the left hand point **(Fig. 1)**.

Check to be sure that the cast on edge has not twisted around the needle. If it has, it is impossible to untwist it. The only way to fix this is to rip it out and return to the cast on row.

Fig. 1a

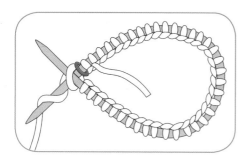

USING TWO CIRCULAR NEEDLES

One method of working in the round, is to use two circular needles at the same time, dividing the stitches equally between both. Each needle is used independently of the other. While you are knitting across the first half of stitches with the other end of the same needle, the second needle will hang out of the way, with the stitches at the center of the cable. Then you will pick up both ends of the second needle, and work across it while the first needle hangs.

To begin, cast on the required number of stitches and slip the last half of stitches onto the second circular needle, placing them at the center of the cable **(Fig. 1b)**. Push the sts on the first needle to the tip at the other end.

A marker can be placed around any stitch to mark first needle.

Move the first needle so that it is in front of and parallel to the cable of the second needle **(Fig. 1c)**. Holding both needles in your left hand, straighten your stitches so that they're not twisted around the needles.

When going from one needle to the next, keep the yarn between the first and last stitches snug to prevent a hole.

Using the other end of the same needle, work across the first needle.

Slide the stitches to the center of the cable and turn your work. Slide the stitches that are on the second needle from the cable to the point and work across. Continue in same manner **(Fig. 1d)**.

Fig. 1b   Fig. 1c

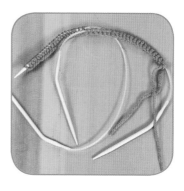 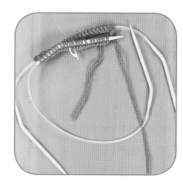

Fig. 1d

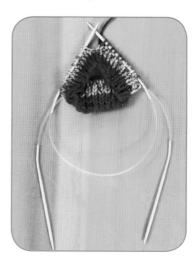

DOUBLE POINTED NEEDLES

The stitches are divided evenly between three (*Fig. 2a*) or four double pointed needles as specified in the individual pattern. Form a triangle or a square with the needles (*Figs. 2b & c*).

Do **not** twist the cast on ridge. With the remaining needle, work across the stitches on the first needle. You will now have an empty needle with which to work the stitches from the next needle. Work the first stitch of each needle firmly to prevent gaps. Continue working around without turning the work.

Fig. 2a

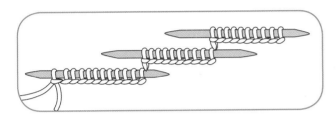

Fig. 2b

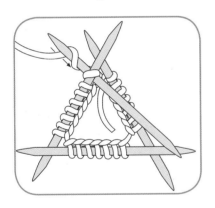

Fig. 2c

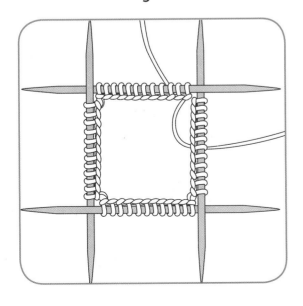

CHANGING COLORS

Wind small amounts of each color onto a bobbin to keep the different color yarns from tangling. You'll need one bobbin for each color change, except when there are so few stitches of the new color that it would be easier to carry the unused color **loosely** across the back (*Fig. 3a*). Always keep the bobbins on the **wrong** side of the garment. When changing colors, always pick up the new color yarn from **beneath** the dropped yarn and keep the color which has just been worked to the left (*Fig. 3b*). This will prevent holes in the finished piece. Take extra care to keep your tension even. For proper fit, it is essential to maintain gauge when following Charts.

Fig. 3a

Fig. 3b

THROUGH BACK LOOP (*abbreviated tbl*)

When instructed to knit or purl into the back loop of a stitch (*Fig. 4*), the result will be twisted stitches.

Fig. 4

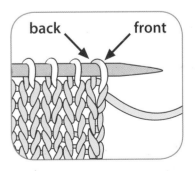

YARN OVERS *(abbreviated YO)*

A Yarn Over *(abbreviated YO)* is simply placing the yarn over the right needle creating an extra stitch. Since the Yarn Over does produce a hole in the knit fabric, it can be used for a lacy effect or a buttonhole. On the row following a Yarn Over, you must be careful to keep it on the needle and treat it as a stitch by knitting or purling it as instructed.

To make a yarn over, you'll loop the yarn over the right needle like you would to knit or purl a stitch, bringing it either to the front or the back of the piece so that it'll be ready to work the next stitch, creating a new stitch on the needle as follows:

After a knit stitch, before a knit stitch
Bring the yarn forward **between** the needles, then back **over** the top of the right hand needle, so that it is now in position to knit the next stitch *(Fig. 5a)*.

Fig. 5a

After a purl stitch, before a purl stitch
Take the yarn **over** the right hand needle to the back, then forward **under** it, so that it is now in position to purl the next stitch *(Fig. 5b)*.

Fig. 5b

After a knit stitch, before a purl stitch
Bring the yarn forward **between** the needles, then back **over** the top of the right hand needle and forward between the needles again, so that it is now in position to purl the next stitch *(Fig. 5c)*.

Fig. 5c

After a purl stitch, before a knit stitch
Take the yarn **over** the right hand needle to the back, so that it is now in position to knit the next stitch *(Fig. 5d)*.

Fig. 5d

ADDING NEW STITCHES

Insert the right needle into the stitch as if to **knit**, yarn over and pull the loop through *(Fig. 6a)*, insert the left needle into the loop just worked from **front** to **back** and slip the loop onto the left needle *(Fig. 6b)*. Repeat for required number of stitches.

Fig. 6a

Fig. 6b

INCREASING EVENLY

Add one to the number of increases required and divide that number into the number of stitches on the needle. Subtract one from the result and the new number is the approximate number of stitches to be worked between each increase. Adjust the number as needed.

KNIT INCREASE

Knit the next stitch but do **not** slip the old stitch off the left needle *(Fig. 7a)*. Insert the right needle into the **back** loop of the **same** stitch and knit it *(Fig. 7b)*, then slip the old stitch off the left needle.

Fig. 7a

Fig. 7b

INVISIBLE INCREASE

Insert the right needle from the **front** into the side of the stitch **below** the next stitch on the left needle *(Fig. 8)* and knit it, then knit the next stitch.

Fig. 8

PURL INCREASE

Purl the next stitch but do **not** slip the old stitch off the left needle. Insert the right needle into the **back** loop of the **same** stitch *(Fig. 9)* and purl it, then slip the old stitch off the left needle.

Fig. 9

MAKE ONE (abbreviated M1)

Insert the left needle under the horizontal strand between the stitches from the front (*Fig. 10a*). Then knit into the back of the strand (*Fig. 10b*).

Fig. 10a

Fig. 10b

DECREASES
KNIT 2 TOGETHER (abbreviated K2 tog)

Insert the right needle into the **front** of the first two stitches on the left needle as if to **knit** (*Fig. 11*), then **knit** them together as if they were one stitch.

Fig. 11

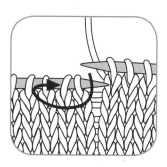

KNIT 2 TOGETHER THROUGH BACK LOOP
(abbreviated K2 tog through back loop)

Insert the right needle into the **back** of the first two stitches on the left needle as if to **knit** (*Fig. 12*), then **knit** them together as if they were one stitch.

Fig. 12

SLIP, SLIP, KNIT (abbreviated SSK)

Slip the first stitch as if to **knit**, then slip the next stitch as if to **knit** (*Fig. 13a*). Insert the **left** needle into the **front** of both slipped stitches (*Fig. 13b*) and knit them together as if they were one stitch (*Fig. 13c*).

Fig. 13a

Fig. 13b

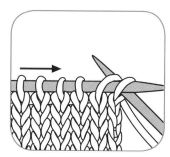

Fig. 13c

SLIP 1, KNIT 1, PASS SLIPPED STITCH OVER
(abbreviated slip 1, K1, PSSO)

Slip one stitch as if to **knit** *(Fig. 14a)*. Knit the next stitch. With the left needle, bring the slipped stitch over the knit stitch just made *(Fig. 14b)* and off the needle.

Fig. 14a   **Fig. 14b**

   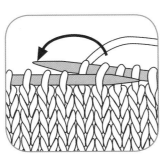

SLIP 1, KNIT 2, PASS SLIPPED STITCH OVER
(abbreviated slip 1, K2, PSSO)

Slip one stitch as if to **knit**. Knit the next two stitches. With the left needle, bring the slipped stitch over the two stitches just made *(Fig. 15)* and off the needle.

Fig. 15

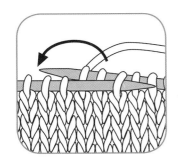

SLIP 1, KNIT 2 TOGETHER, PASS SLIPPED STITCH OVER
(abbreviated slip 1, K2 tog, PSSO)

Slip one stitch as if to **knit**. Knit the next two stitches together *(Fig. 11, page 196)*. With the left needle, bring the slipped stitch over the stitch just made *(Fig. 16)* and off the needle.

Fig. 16

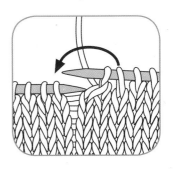

SLIP 2 TOGETHER, KNIT 1, PASS 2 SLIPPED STITCHES OVER
(abbreviated slip 2 tog, K1, P2SSO)

Slip two stitches together as if to **knit**. Knit the next stitch. With the left needle, bring the 2 slipped stitches over the stitch just made *(Fig. 17)* and off the needle.

Fig. 17

PURL 2 TOGETHER (abbreviated P2 tog)

Insert the right needle into the **front** of the first two stitches on the left needle as if to **purl** (*Fig. 18*), then **purl** them together as if they were one stitch.

Fig. 18

PURL 2 TOGETHER THROUGH BACK LOOP
(abbreviated P2 tog tbl)

Insert the right needle into the **back** of the second, then the first stitch on the left needle as if to **purl** (*Fig. 19*), then **purl** them together as if they were one stitch.

Fig. 19

PURL 3 TOGETHER (abbreviated P3 tog)

Insert the right needle into the **front** of the first three stitches on the left needle as if to **purl** (*Fig. 20*), then **purl** them together as if they were one stitch.

Fig. 20

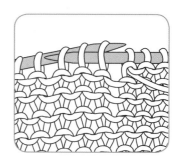

SLIP, SLIP, PURL (abbreviated SSP)

Slip the first stitch as if to **knit**, then slip the next stitch as if to **knit**. Place these two stitches back onto the left needle. Insert the **right** needle into the **back** of both slipped stitches from the **back** to **front** (*Fig. 21*) and purl them together as if they were one stitch.

Fig. 21

PICKING UP STITCHES

When instructed to pick up stitches, insert the needle from the **front** to the **back** under two strands at the edge of the worked piece *(Fig. 22a or b)*. Put the yarn around the needle as if to **knit**, then bring the needle with the yarn back through the stitch to the right side, resulting in a stitch on the needle.

Repeat this along the edge, picking up the required number of stitches.

A crochet hook may be helpful to pull yarn through.

Fig. 22a

Fig. 22b

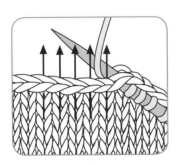

WEAVING SEAMS

With the **right** side of both pieces facing you and edges even, sew through both pieces once to secure the beginning of the seam, leaving an ample yarn end to weave in later. Insert the needle under the bar **between** the first and second stitches on the row and pull the yarn through *(Fig. 23)*. Insert the needle under the next bar on the second side. Repeat from side to side, being careful to match rows. If the edges are different lengths, it may be necessary to insert the needle under two bars at one edge.

Fig. 23

WHIPSTITCH SEAMS

With **right** sides together, sew through both pieces once to secure the beginning of the seam, leaving an ample yarn end to weave in later. Insert the needle from **front** to **back** through two strands on each piece *(Fig. 24)*. Bring the needle around and insert it from front to back through the next two strands on both pieces. Repeat along the edge.

Fig. 24

GRAFTING

Thread the yarn needle with the long end. Hold the threaded yarn needle on the right side of work. Work in the following sequence, pulling yarn through as if to knit or as if to purl with even tension and keeping yarn under points of needles to avoid tangling and extra loops.

Step 1: Purl first stitch on **front** needle, leave on *(Fig. 25a)*.
Step 2: Knit first stitch on **back** needle, leave on *(Fig. 25b)*.
Step 3: Knit first stitch on **front** needle, slip off.
Step 4: Purl next stitch on **front** needle, leave on.
Step 5: Purl first stitch on **back** needle, slip off.
Step 6: Knit next stitch on **back** needle, leave on.
Repeat Steps 3-6 across until one stitch remains on each needle, then repeat Steps 3 and 5.

Fig. 25a

Fig. 25b

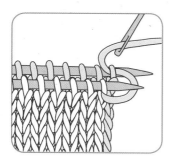

3-NEEDLE BIND OFF

Holding pieces with **right** sides together and needles parallel to each other, insert a third needle as if to **knit** into the first stitch on the front needle **and** into the first stitch on the back needle *(Fig. 26)*. Knit these two stitchess together and slip them off the needles, ★ knit the next stitch on each needle together and slip them off the needles. To bind off, insert one left needle into the first stitch on the right needle and pull the first stitch over the second stitch and off the right needle; repeat from ★ across until all of the stitches have been bound off.

Fig. 26

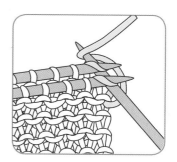

BLOCKING

Blocking helps to smooth your work and give it a professional appearance. Check the yarn label for any special instructions about blocking.

With acrylics that can be blocked, place your project on a clean terry towel over a flat surface and pin in place to the desired size using rust-proof pins where needed. Cover it with dampened bath towels. When the towels are dry, the project is blocked.

If the yarn is hand washable, carefully launder your project using a mild soap or detergent, being careful to gently squeeze suds through the piece. Rinse it several times in cool, clear water without wringing or twisting. Remove any excess moisture by rolling it in a succession of dry terry towels. You can put it in the final spin cycle of your washer, without water. Lay the project on a large towel on a flat surface out of direct sunlight. Gently smooth and pat it to the desired size and shape. When it is completely dry, it is blocked.

Another method of blocking, that is especially good for wool, requires a steam iron or a handheld steamer. Place your project on a clean terry towel over a flat surface and shape; pin in place using rust-proof pins where needed. Hold a steam iron or steamer just above the item and steam it thoroughly. Never let the weight of the iron touch the item because it will flatten the stitches. Leave the item pinned until it is completely dry.

FRINGE

Cut a piece of cardboard 6" (15 cm) wide and half as long as the required strands. Wind the yarn loosely and evenly around the cardboard until the card is filled, then cut across one end; repeat as needed. Hold together as many strands as specified in the individual instructions; fold in half. With wrong side facing and using a crochet hook, draw the folded end up through a stitch and pull the loose ends through the folded end (*Fig. 27a*); draw the knot up tightly (*Fig. 27b*). Repeat, spacing as specified in individual instructions. Lay Shawl on a hard surface and trim the ends.

POM-POM

Cut a piece of cardboard 3" (7.5 cm) wide and as long as you want the diameter of your finished pom-pom to be.

Wind the yarn around the cardboard until it is approximately ¹/₂" (12 mm) thick in the middle (*Fig. 28a*). Carefully slip the yarn off the cardboard and firmly tie an 18" (45.5 cm) length of yarn around the middle (*Fig. 28b*). Leave yarn ends long enough to attach the pom-pom. Cut the loops on both ends and trim the pom-pom into a smooth ball (*Fig. 28c*).

Fig. 28a

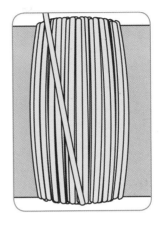

Fig. 28b

Fig. 27a

Fig. 27b

Fig. 28c

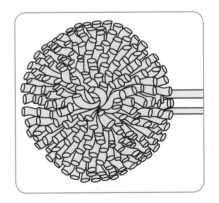

DUPLICATE STITCH

Thread a tapestry needle with an 18" (45.5 cm) length of yarn. Each square on the chart represents one knit stitch. Each knit stitch forms a V. With **right** side facing, bring the needle up from the wrong side at the base of the V, leaving an end to be woven in later. The needle should always go between the strands of yarn. Follow the right side of the V up and insert the needle from right to left under the legs of the V immediately above it, keeping the yarn on top of the stitch *(Fig. 29a)*, and draw through. Follow the left side of the V back down to the base and insert the needle back through the bottom of the same stitch where the first stitch began *(Fig. 29b, Duplicate Stitch completed)*.

Continuing to follow the chart, repeat for each stitch, keeping tension even with tension of knit fabric to avoid puckering.

When a length of yarn is finished, run it under several stitches on back of work to secure.

Fig. 29a	Fig. 29b

FELTING

MACHINE FELTING

Use ONLY a top-loading washer.
Use the HOT wash setting with a COLD rinse cycle.
DO NOT LET IT SPIN. This can cause creases that don't come out.

Our model was felted using 1 tablespoon of detergent. However, some don't like to use any soap or detergent at all.

Place your Knitted Tote in a tight-mesh sweater bag to contain the fuzz your Tote may shed.
Check your project every 2-3 minutes to monitor for size and shrinkage. When you check your Tote, wear rubber gloves to protect your hands. Be careful, the water is very hot. If your Tote has not felted enough by the end of the wash cycle, repeat as needed and continue to check your Tote frequently.

If your Tote is left in the hot water too long, it can become too small and the fabric too tight.
We do NOT recommend putting felted projects in the dryer. They will continue to shrink and shed and change their shape.

BLOCKING

Block IMMEDIATELY. Remove your Tote from the sweater bag and roll it in a towel and gently squeeze out the excess water. DO NOT WRING.

Form it into the size and shape you want by pulling and patting.

Place a plastic grocery bag inside-out over a foam board block. This is used to make it easier to pull the felted Tote over the block. Place the Tote over the end of the foam board and pull downward until the entire Tote is on the block. Place plastic wrap around the block if the felt will no longer slide.

Let your Tote air dry; it may take several days.

BASIC CROCHET STITCHES

YARN OVER *(abbreviated YO)*

Bring the yarn over the top of the hook from back to front, catching the yarn with the hook and turning the hook slightly toward you to keep the yarn from slipping off *(Fig. 30)*.

Fig. 30

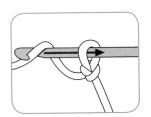

SINGLE CROCHET

Insert hook in stitch indicated, YO and pull up a loop, YO and draw through both loops on hook *(Fig. 31)*.

Fig. 31

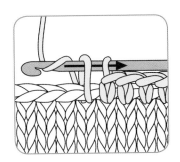

DOUBLE CROCHET

YO, insert hook in stitch indicated, YO and pull up a loop, (YO and draw through 2 loops on hook) twice *(Figs. 32a & b)*.

Fig. 32a

Fig. 32b

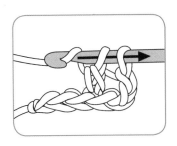

JOINING WITH SC

Begin with a slip knot on the hook. Insert hook in stitch indicated, YO and pull up a loop *(Fig. 33a)*, YO and draw through both loops on hook *(Fig. 33b)*.

Fig. 33a

Fig. 33b

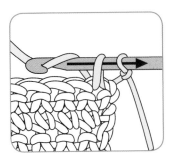
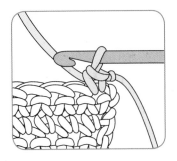

SLIP STITCH

Insert hook in stitch indicated, YO and draw through stitch and through loop on hook *(Fig. 34)*.

Fig. 34

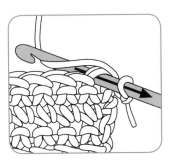

yarn information

The projects in this leaflet were made using a variety of yarns. Any brand in the specified weight may be used. It is best to refer to the yardage/meters when determining how many skeins or balls to purchase. Remember, to arrive at the finished size, it is the GAUGE/TENSION that is important, not the brand of yarn. For your convenience, listed below are the specific yarns used to create our photography models.

TWO-TONE THROW
Patons® Shetland Chunky
#03022 Taupe
#03040 Black

SCULPTURED PILLOWS
Cascade Yarns, 220 Heathers
#2437 (Tan)

PRETTY PANELS AFGHAN
Lion Brand® Jiffy®
Rose - #137 Blush
Brown - #122 Caffé

KEEPSAKE DOILY
Coats® Aunt Lydia's® Classic Crochet Thread
#226 Natural

SPA CLOTH & SOAP SACK
Bernat® Handicrafter® Cotton
#00030 Pale Yellow

GARTER STITCH SQUARES
Patons® Classic Wool
#226 Black
#201 Winter White

SPRINGTIME PULLOVER
Cascade Yarns, Cherub Collection DK
#28 Pink
#32 Purple
#24 Yellow
#31 Green

BOATS FOR CAMERON
Lion Brand® Chunky USA
White - #100 Snowcap White
Blue - #106 Pacific Blue

BABY BLOCKS
Bernat® Satin
#04420 Sea Shell

A LESSON ON COLOR
Lion Brand® Micro Spun
Purple - #147 Purple
Green - #194 Lime
Turquoise - #148 Turquoise
Coral - #103 Coral

WELCOME, LITTLE ONESIE
Berroco's Wendy Peter Pan Spot Print DK
Spot Print - #772 Iced Gateau
Berroco's Wendy Peter Pan DK
Peach - #302 Peach Cream
Mint - #304 Watersprite
Yellow - #303 Pale Lemon
Blue - #306 Baby Blue

BABY BONNET
Patons® Astra
#02943 Maize Yellow

BABY'S HOODED CARDIGAN
Berroco's Wendy Peter Pan DK
White - #300 Pure White
Baby Blue - #306 Baby Blue
Pale Yellow - #303 Pale Lemon
Peach - #302 Peach Cream
Lt Green - #304 Watersprite
Lavender - #307 Slumberland
Baby Pink - #305 Baby Pink

FELTED KNITTING TOTE
Patons® Classic Wool, Merino
#00240 Leaf Green
#00202 Aran
#77732 That's Pink

CABLE SAMPLER SCARF
Fiber Trends Inc.
Naturally Yarns Harmony
#700 Aran

FRANCO'S MUFFLER
Misti Alpaca Chunky
#100 Natural Cream

SEATTLE CHILL CHASERS
Bernat® Berella "4"®
#08940 Natural

PONCHO
Caron® Country
#0013 Spruce

HOODED SCARF
Red Heart® Soft Baby Steps™
Main Color - #9800 Baby Blue
Contrasting Color - #9932 Puppy Print

FAIR ISLE HAT & SCARF
Bernat® Softee® Baby
Pink - #30205 Prettiest Pink
Variegated - #30301 Baby Pink Marls
White - #2000 White
Red Heart® Sport
Dk Pink - #922 Hot Pink

CUFFED HAT
Cascade Yarns, Cascade 220
#7813 Jade

A LITTLE SOMETHING FOR YOU
TLC® Cotton Plus™
#3100 Cream

COWL
**Universal Yarn® Debbie Macomber
Blossom Street™ Collection, Wild Meadow**
#306 Juneau

A WISP OF WARMTH
Knit Picks® Alpaca Cloud
#23499 Peppermint Heather

ALWAYS WITH YOU
Lion Brand® Vanna's Choice®
Rose - #140 Dusty Rose
Purple - #146 Dusty Purple
Patons® Decor
Brown - #01632 Rich Taupe

REESE'S VEST
Knit Picks® Andean Treasure Yarn
#23488 Granite Heather

CABLE SLIPPERS
**Premier™ Yarns Deborah Norville Collection,
Everyday™ Soft Worsted**
#ED100-10 Aubergine

SOCKS
Bernat® Sox
#42013 Desert Storm

HANNAH'S ANKLE SOCKS
Red Heart® Heart & Sole™
Main Color - #3970 Faded Jeans
Contrasting Color - #3115 Ivory

THICK SOCKS
Cascade Yarns, Cascade 220
#8901 Groseille

RIBBED TURTLENECK
Plymouth Yarn® Baby Alpaca Grande
#403 Grey Heather
On Line Cocoon
#03 Brindle

LEIF'S SWEATER
**Fancy Image Yarn DK
Machine Washable Merino Wool**
#39132 Medium Blue

JOLENE'S PULLOVER
Caron® Simply Soft®
#9748 Rubin Red

BAXTER'S COZY COAT
Lion Brand® Vanna's Choice®
#173 Dusty Green

BEADED WEDDING SET
**Jade Sapphire Exotic Fibres,
Mongolian Cashmere 2-ply**
#000 Ivory

POSITIVELY PRETTY PULLOVER
Moda-Dea® Bamboo Wool™
#3920 Chili Pepper Red

CODY'S DINOSAUR SWEATER
Red Heart® Classic™
Main color - #822 True Blue
Brown - #339 Mild Brown

HARVEY'S VEST
Patons® Classic Wool
#00208 Burgundy

a word from Leisure Arts and MIRA Books

Look for Debbie's heartwarming stories at bookstores everywhere, and collect all eleven of her knitting publications!

knit along with
DEBBIE MACOMBER

Read the books that inspired the projects.

Cedar Cove Series

Inspired by Debbie's popular Blossom Street and Cedar Cove book series, the *Knit Along with Debbie Macomber* companion books are a treasure trove of patterns to knit and crochet! And have you discovered the classic knit patterns in *Debbie's Favorites* or the thoughtful designs in *Friendship Shawls* and *A Charity Guide for Knitters*? Take time to indulge yourself with Debbie's heartwarming tales; then treat yourself to a world of creativity from Leisure Arts!

Item # 4658

Blossom Street Series

Item # 5506

Item # 5121

Item # 4600

Item # 4729

Item # 4279

Item # 4135

Item # 4132

Other Debbie Macomber Publications